BLOOMSBURY GUIDE TO BETTER WRITING

BLOOMSBURY GUIDE TO

Letter Writing

NIGEL REES

B L O O M S B U R Y

First published in 1994 by Bloomsbury Publishing Plc,
2 Soho Square, London W1V 5DE

This paperback edition first published in 1995

A copy of the CIP entry for this book is available
upon request from the British Library

ISBN 0 7475 1430 5

10 9 8 7 6 5 4 3 2 1

Designed by Geoff Green
Typeset by Hewer Text Composition Services, Edinburgh
Printed and bound by Cox & Wyman Ltd, Reading, Berks

Contents

CONTENTS

INTRODUCTION

London, 1994

Dear Reader,

It should be as great a pleasure to write letters as it is to receive them. Alas, many people do not find that this is so. For them, writing a letter is not an enjoyable task, but one frequently to be postponed and only to be accomplished at the last possible moment, if at all. This book is for them, in particular, as well as for those who do not find letter writing a burden but who would like to make their letters more effective.

The *Bloomsbury Guide to Letter Writing* is a companion volume to my earlier *Bloomsbury Guide to Good Manners* – which was originally published as *Best Behaviour* in 1992. That book does contain a chapter on 'Written Communication', as well as dealing fully with such practical matters as addressing titled people in 'Titles and Addressing'. The present book expands that earlier material, provides guidance and tips, and describes what is considered to be 'correct form' in this field, while frequently challenging that form and indicating instead what you may be able to get away with.

In common with its companion volume, the *Bloomsbury Guide to Letter Writing* also contains an entertaining selection of comments and quotable remarks that have been made over the years on various aspects of its subject, both for and against.

[Mrs Millamant:] 'O ay, letters – I had letters – I am persecuted with letters – I hate letters – nobody knows how to write letters; and yet one has 'em, one does not know why – they serve one to pin up one's hair.' – William Congreve, *The Way of the World* (1700)

'Those who are absent, by [the post's] means become present; it is the consolation of life.' – Voltaire, 'Post', *Philosophical Dictionary* (1764)

'An odd thought strikes me: – we shall receive no letters in the grave.' –
Samuel Johnson, in Boswell's *Life of Johnson* (regarding December 1784)

'I have received no more than one or two letters in my life that were worth
the postage.' – Henry David Thoreau, *Walden* (1854)

'A letter is an unannounced visit, and the postman is thus the agent of
impolite surprises. Every week we ought to have an hour for receiving
letters – and then go and take a bath.' – F.W. Nietzsche, *Human All-too-
Human* (1878)

'Letter-writing: that most delightful way of wasting time.' – John Morley
(1838-1923), *The Life of George Eliot*

'Letters for the rich, letters for the poor,
The shop at the corner, the girl next door . . .
Letters of thanks, letters from banks,
Letters of joy from girl and boy . . .
And applications for situations,
And timid lovers' declarations,
And gossip, gossip from all the nations.' – W.H. Auden, *Night Mail* (1936)

I genuinely enjoy receiving letters of all kinds, even though – or
especially as – these days good letters are the tiny amount of gold
that I manage to filter out of the mass of bills and junk mail that daily
pours through my letter box. Despite all this, a letter still remains
something special. It is tangible; it is not forgotten as soon as it is
finished (like a phone call); it is a small fragment of the sender's person
that you can always keep, should you wish to, and call your own.

With this enjoyment goes intense anticipation of the post's arrival,
acute disappointment if it fails to bring any genuine letters, and raging
fury if you suspect that an awaited missive has been put through the
wrong letter box. Few situations make you feel as helpless as this one.

Sending letters is, on the other hand, an act of creation just as much as
writing a book or an article, even if what you are putting down on paper
is only a complaint to your bank manager. Added to this, the ritual of
taking your letter to the post box is not without its significance and,
even, satisfaction.

It is unfortunate that letter writing sometimes gets a bad press, but
this is usually because complainers make the mistake of confusing the
content of unwelcome letters with the practice of letter writing as a
whole. If we were to exclude correspondence from our ideal society it
would be because it represented business, legal and office matters – and

we would be quite right to exclude all that. But there is more to letter writing than this.

What I have tried to do in this book is to make the process of writing letters that much easier by passing on my own experience in many different types of correspondence, by quoting from successful and entertaining letters of the past, and by providing sample material – in some cases entire specimen letters – which may be adapted for your own purposes.

Above all, I have tried, by surveying the whole field of letter writing (which includes the unexpected areas of chain letters, fan letters and hate mail), to help the reader see the value, pleasure and purpose of correspondence. In fact, the *Guide to Letter Writing* is rather more than a 'How to . . .' book; it is as well a celebration of the art of letter writing in all its many forms.

*

As always, I am indebted to many people – almost all of them ace correspondents – who have aided and abetted me in my task. Kathy Rooney and Kate Newman (who proposed the book) at Bloomsbury Publishing are shining examples of those who have rediscovered the pleasures of the handwritten letter following the invention of the fax machine (though I have to say that the handwriting of one is a good deal easier to decipher than the other . . .). I have received advice, information, cooperation and encouragement from many people, including: Donald Hickling; Jean Farrugia, Chief Archivist of the Post Office in London; Thomas J.P. Sexton; Penny Rees; James W.S. Rees. I am also most grateful – for showing me the way – to all those correspondents whose letters I have reworked in order that they may become useful illustrations.

*

Publications I have consulted include:

The Faber Book of Letters, ed. Felix Pryor, Faber & Faber, 1988
From Pillar to Post – The Troubled History of the Mail, Laurin Zilliacus, William Heinemann, 1956
The Great Diurnall of Nicholas Blundell 3 vols, ed. Frank Tyrer, The Record Society of Lancashire and Cheshire, 1968-72

The Guinness Book of Autographs, Ray Rawlins, Guinness Superlatives Ltd, 1977

The Oxford English Dictionary (Second Edition), Oxford University Press, 1989

The Story of the Pony Express, Raymond and Mary Settle, W. Foulsham & Co., 1955

Trollope, Victoria Glendinning, Hutchinson, 1992

*

How to use the specimen letters

In the course of this book I quote from a number of actual letters, as well as providing specimen, made-up letters to illustrate the points I am trying to make. Just a word on this aspect of the book. The specimen letters are intended as a *guide* and no more. They are not intended to be copied out word for word – merely to provide you with a structure and some ideas, phraseology and so on for your own letters. It would be ill-advised for you to copy out any of these letters in their entirety. They are meant to be edited and adapted for your own purposes. Besides, the whole point of a letter is to convey the personality and spontaneity of expression of the writer. By their very nature, specimen letters can do neither of things. They are given merely to prompt and encourage. In other words, shake well before using.

And please note: In the specimen letters, names, addresses, post codes, telephone numbers and account numbers have been included, where appropriate, to give a greater touch of authenticity. These are all invented and, in the event of any duplication with or resemblance to real-life counterparts, no connection should be made with the content of the specimen letters.

With best wishes,

Yours sincerely,

Nigel Rees

∞ 1 ∞

MAIL SUPREMACY

Rather than delve into a detailed – and rather dry – history of the postal services, it would be best, for our present purposes, to assume that letters of one sort or another have always existed. What *has* changed over the millennia is the way they have been delivered and the tools with which they have been made. The latter aspect, in particular, has had a profound effect on the nature of the missive. The technology continues to change (and yes, I think, improve) so that we are now well into an era of electronic mail which does not require any form of the traditional 'pen and paper' and even does away with direct human participation in delivery. This takes away much of the letter experience – the feel of the paper, the look of the handwriting, the slitting open of the envelope – but, for good or ill, it makes us review fundamental changes in the style and substance of correspondence.

To whom it may concern

Why do we write letters? Because we wish to communicate with another person who is physically apart from us. Much more importantly, however, we write letters because the process of *putting down on paper* what we want to tell that person is more effective than speaking it. Writing a letter allows for more consideration on the part of the sender and more consideration on the part of the receiver. In some situations it can also, of course, allow a more intimate approach to the mind of the recipient than spoken communication would allow. And if not more intimate, then at least it can be a more powerful and effective communication than the spoken word.

From year zero until the nineteenth century letters were sent by messenger, however great or small the distance that was to be covered. In ancient times the messenger might have carried the letter in a cleft stick, and run or walked or ridden a horse. Using an individual messenger to carry your letter had the inestimable advantage – one recalls rather fondly in these days of shrinking postal services – that the writer could send a letter at any hour of the day or night provided a messenger could be found and the cost could be borne.

By the sixteenth and seventeenth centuries it was possible to discern quite elaborate postal services carrying letters in bulk, and not just from one sender. In Britain letters were taken over longer distances by a network of messengers who road 'post horses' which ran in relays along 'post-roads', and these eventually gave their name to the system of carrying the mails (rather than the other way round). *The Oxford English Dictionary* (2nd edition) defines one meaning of the word *post* as 'from the beginning of the 16th c., applied to men with horses stationed or appointed in places at suitable distances along the post-roads, the duty of each being to ride with, or forward with all speed to the next stage, the king's "packet", and at length the letters of other persons.'

('Post' has always been the predominant term in Britain, whereas 'mail' became more popular in the United States. The 'Royal Mail' in Britain still uses the term for the organization, however, and has done since the service was inaugurated in 1635, but 'Post Office' is probably most people's preferred term these days.)

The cost of carrying mail in this way was according to the distance it had to be carried. The odd feature of the first attempts at organization was the fact that the *receiver* of the letter rather than the sender had to pay for it. As one might expect, there are plenty of stories of letters being refused on account of the cost, as well as of large sums of money being handed over to carriers for letters which turned out to be a disappointment.

Prepaid penny post

In 1840 Sir Rowland Hill invented the *prepaid* penny postal system, which meant that the *sender* of the letter bore the cost. This had the incidental effect of the appearance of letter boxes in front doors because the deliverer no longer had to wait and collect payment. As a result of Hill's innovation, the number of letters posted almost trebled within the next twenty-four months. Then, soon after, mail started to be carried around the country even more speedily by railway train.

The rest of the nineteenth century in the British Isles saw the rapid spread of a highly efficient postal system involving multiple daily collections and deliveries of mail, including same-day deliveries in some places. The gradual erosion of this superb service in the mid-twentieth century is a cause of great regret, though as we near the end of the century, the combined effect of electronic mail, faxes, bike messengers, express delivery services and the possibility of an end to the Post Office's monopoly has almost created a nearly acceptable substitute system.

A social historian could have a field day considering what the precise effects of having a major postal system have been. Victoria Glendinning in her biography of the novelist Anthony Trollope (who also worked in the Post Office for many years) suggests that 'it was commercial houses and the middle class who chiefly availed themselves of the new service. The penny post speeded up business transactions, friendships and love affairs. It opened up new possibilities of intensity and a whole new field of anguish.' And she quotes from Trollope's novel *The Claverings* (1867) in which Florence Burton frets because she has not heard from her lover. Her brother says to his wife: 'I used to think myself the best lover in the world, if I wrote once a month.' 'There was no penny post then, Mr Burton,' the wife points out. Says he, 'And I often wish there was none now.'

The mail must get through

The importance of carrying out deliveries and of surmounting any obstacles to them has always been paramount in any organized postal service. Jean Farrugia, Chief Archivist of the Post Office in London, points out that this 'reflects a tradition that goes back centuries. . . . By the time of the Tudors it was not uncommon for letters sent by the Royal Mail service to bear on the outside the sign of the gallows to support such endorsements as "Haste, Post, haste, haste for Life . . ."

'Indeed, those carrying the Royal Mail have died in their efforts to get it through at all costs. Examples of this exist in the history of the Post Office Packet Service (whose captains' standing instructions were to "run where you can and to stand and fight when you can no longer run") and in that of the Mail Coach service (whose Guards, should a coach become stuck fast in the snow, would struggle onwards with the Mail either on horseback or even on foot). A notable example of this was the Guard of the Edinburgh Mail who sacrificed his life in a vain attempt to get the mail through [in 1831].'

The precise slogan 'the mail must get through' (or 'go through') would appear to have originated in the United States in connection with the somewhat short-lived Pony Express mail delivery service. In April 1860, for example, the arrival in Sacramento, California, of the first Pony Express delivery – a satchel with forty-nine letters and three newspapers that had left St Joseph, Missouri, eleven days previously, was greeted as an astounding improvement over the eight-week wagon convoys previously used. The brave riders vowed 'the mail must get through' despite all kinds of dangers, ranging from hostile Indians on the prairie to storms in the mountains. But they were to be overtaken quite soon by the 'Iron Horse', as railroads gradually extended all over the country, and by the rapid spread of the electric telegraph.

Mail delivery in the United States is latterly sometimes said to have been conducted at a less heroic level. I can but recall the inscription from Herodotus which can be seen over the General Post Office in New York. It goes, 'Neither snow nor rain nor heat nor gloom of night stays these couriers from the swift completion of their appointed rounds.' To which someone made the obvious rejoinder, 'Well, what is it, then?'

Capital letters

Whatever the difficulties in conveying written messages from sender to receiver, their superiority over modern spoken communications is unquestionable. It is a truism that letters are more effective than telephone calls in conveying what they have to. It is, of course, easier to chatter on the phone than to put pen to paper, but there is nothing left to show for a phone call at the end of it other than the bill. This should be a cause of concern not only to biographers and others who now find that the rich revelations of personal correspondence are now largely denied them.

'In a man's letters his soul lies naked.' – Samuel Johnson, letter to Hester Thrale (27 October 1777)

'When I began this letter I thought I had something to say: but I believe the truth was I had nothing to do.' – Edward Fitzgerald (1809-83)

'Any man who does not write books, has plenty of time to think, and lives in unsatisfying society, is likely to be a good letter-writer.' – F.W. Nietzsche, *Human All-too-Human* (1878)

'There are certain people whom one almost feels inclined to urge to hurry up and die so that their letters can be published.' – Christopher Morley (1890-1957)

'[Published] letters by a living man are a bit like a stately home with the owner around – one isn't sure how much one can touch.' – Wilfrid Sheed, *The Good Word* (1978)

'We may be the last generation to write to each other.' – Philip Larkin to Judy Egerton, a friend of thirty years, in 1981. (A selection of Larkin's letters was published in 1992.)

The nature of written correspondence – whether superior to spoken communication or not – has itself been affected by several major changes in the technology. The invention of the *modern* fountain pen by Lewis Edson Waterman took place around 1883. Waterman created a special device for slowing down the ink feed to the nib and thus reduced the chance of any leaking. Consequently, the centuries-old dipping of quill pen into inkpot was finally made redundant. There had been fountain pens (that is, pens with a reservoir of ink attached) since the early eighteenth century, but this was the breakthrough. The result? Writing became a faster activity. But could it be that thinking time was reduced proportionately?

J.C. Prince celebrated the invention of the new version in 'The Pen and the Press', included in *The Thousand Best Poems in the World* (1891):

It came as a boon and blessing to men,
The peaceful, the pure, the victorious PEN!

(In turn, this became a slogan for the pens manufactured by MacNiven and H. Cameron Ltd in the 1920s:

They come as a boon and a blessing to men,
The Pickwick, the Owl, and the Waverley pen.)

In 1943 came the patenting of the 'biro' capillary attraction system – a method of writing with quick-drying ink, using a ballpoint rather than a conventional nib, which is the basis of all ballpoint pens today. There actually was a Mr Biro – László Biró (*d*. 1985) – a Hungarian who settled in Argentina in 1940. The success of the pen was helped by its being offered to US and UK forces in the Second World War. It would not leak at high altitudes and could even be used to write under water. The word 'biro' – which is also a brand name – is now often applied indiscriminately to all types of ballpoint and is pronounced to rhyme with 'giro' rather than the original 'hero'. Drawback? It has made writing *too* easy and visually sloppy.

Approximately thirty years later, another highly-significant development took place. 'Dry toner' photocopying began to be used widely in offices, thus putting an end to the messy copying involved in the use of carbon paper, Roneo and Banda machines (the last two of which required fluids). The result? It is probable that a higher value came to be placed on letters, both for their appearance and their contents, because now the sender could retain a version that was as good as the original.

The year 1982 marks the approximate beginning of the popular use of word-processing equipment for private and business correspondence. By this time, too, computer programmes had been introduced for the writing of formula letters, addressing of envelopes and mass mailing. The consequences? Letters took on a generally improved visual appearance. Or, at least, a noticeable decrease in type-written error. However, sometimes content suffered from the ease of computerized composition, and, where certain kinds of dot-matrix printer were used, a different type of visual difficulty was substituted for what may have gone before: the ink looked vague and grey.

The widespread use of fax machines for business and domestic purposes, bringing with it a return to handwritten notes and increased informality in business communication, may be dated to about 1989.

All we want is the fax, ma'am

A fax (properly 'facsimile') machine is an interesting piece of equipment that enables you to send letters by transmitting, as it were, a photo of the letter over an ordinary telephone line. Use of such machines is now widespread in business and not infrequent at a more informal level. Quite apart from the speed with which documents whose visual appearance is important can be sent, there is also the bonus of *being able to deliver your own mail* at the time when you want it to arrive.

The sending of personal messages by fax is one of the most welcome of recent communications developments. It can be a discreet and speedy way of conveying information without having to engage in a full-blown telephone conversation. If you are sending instructions or a map, say, the recipient has something tangible to hold on to. Above all, faxing has an agreeable informality to it, not least when it has encouraged people to return to writing their notes out by hand.

I think one can assume that if other people have fax machines, then they will be happy to receive personal messages on them. It has been known for love letters to be faxed, but on the whole the machine should not be used for thank-you letters or for replying to invitations or for letters of a sensitive nature – unless, of course, the exchange has been initiated by the other person via fax.

Whether for personal or business use, it is important that some form of standard cover note be included with the message to make it very clear who the sender is, who the fax is intended for, and how many pages are being sent. It is worth remembering that faxes may well be received in an open office and read not only by the people they are addressed to. The confidentiality of any information they contain is therefore always at risk.

Junk mail sent by fax is totally unacceptable. It is intrusive and, what is more, it uses up your paper without so much as a by your leave. Senders of junk faxes should be requested to remove your name from their lists. In June 1993 a London court fined a company that had sent 'junk' faxes advertising its services. The prosecution had worked out that whereas it cost an advertiser 59p to send a sheet of material by post, it cost only 27p to send it by fax – the receiver bearing costs of 4p a sheet (covering the fax paper, ink and machine maintenance).

The principle at law seemed to be that unsolicited faxes amounted to trespass for the purpose of advertising and a conversion of materials for the sender's purposes. A number of American states have made junk faxing illegal. It remains to be seen whether junk fax will be included in the 'Telephone Preference Scheme' being established by the Direct Marketing Association, under which people can choose not to receive telesales calls, just as they can choose not to receive junk mail under the Mailing Preference Service (see Chapter 8, page 150).

Should the sending of faxes ever come to compensate us for the loss of the five-deliveries-daily postal services of the nineteenth century – and in their instantaneousness I think they almost have – there is one small snag: fax paper fades, taking with it the messages. The pleasures of coming across old correspondence are thus largely lost to the fax user *unless* a plain paper machine is used or the receiver takes the trouble to photocopy the messages on to more durable paper.

To type or not to type?

The 'handwritten note' is often singled out nowadays as being a rather special form of communication. It is taken as showing that senders are really caring people because they have taken the time and trouble to write *personally*. By doing so they remove any suspicion that a standard, typewritten form of words is being foisted on the recipient, or that a third party might have had a hand in the composition of the letter.

Any encouragement to write letters (or faxes) in longhand must, however, be qualified by an awareness that a writer's handwriting is quite often only legible to that person. If you are aware that your handwriting does give people difficulty, you should seriously consider always typing your letters. There are few things more tedious than having to spend hours deciphering an alien hand. This advice would extend to personal notes – though one would obviously think twice before sending a typewritten love letter or message of thanks, congratulation or condolence (though examples of all these have been known, I assure you). There are ways in which a typed letter can be personalized in the 'topping and tailing' and made less official – as in business correspondence (see page 101). The 'Dear Frances' and the 'Yours ever, Philip' can be handwritten. *Minor* handwritten corrections to the typing can have a positive effect – they show at least that you have cared sufficiently to re-read what you have written before sending it off.

So, it can be all right to type personal notes? Yes, provided you don't do it without thinking. Your first instinct should be for the handwritten note. And yet, I have an uncle who has the most appallingly illegible handwriting in the world; he knows this, and has always typed everything. This, to my mind, is perfectly considerate and courteous to the recipients of his missives. So I am very glad that he does it. If you have any doubts on this score, then an acceptable compromise is to type but also to add a note apologizing for doing so, explaining why you think it is necessary.

Unfortunately, not all people are aware how difficult their handwriting can be to read. No man's handwriting is illegible to himself. It was remarked of the indecipherable hand of the hostess Sybil Colefax that the only way to tell what she was writing to you about was to pin her notes and invitations to the wall and *run* past them.

Which said, I must return to the point that there are fewer things pleasanter to receive than a handwritten letter which is easy to read. The fact that there are practitioners of graphology – the science of reading a people's characters from their handwriting – should not deter you from doing what comes naturally to you.

'Ye see how large a letter I have written unto you with mine own hand.' – St Paul's Epistle to the Galatians, 6:11

Processed pieces

It is a long way from the 'personal note' written 'in your own hand' to what has come to be called 'word processing'. This unfortunate term was coined for the composition of documents using a personal computer. It makes writing a letter sound about as individual an activity as making processed peas on a production line. Indeed, it is reminiscent of that other unfortunate term 'convenience food' (which sounds as if it was meant to be consumed in an inappropriate public place).

But there it is. Many people now write their personal letters on a word processor rather than struggle with a typewriter. The technology of word processing means it is much simpler to clear up your mistakes and to present a smoother end product. In business the new technology may be preferred to the traditional dictating of letters to a secretary, which is a specialized art and can be quite difficult. Whatever the reason for choosing to write letters on a personal computer, it does mean that composition becomes a more direct way of 'putting your thoughts down on paper'. There is no third party involved; indeed, it is just like writing with a pen in your hand, the traditional way.

Other advantages of computerized document production include the possibility of superbly printed letters (particularly if you have access to a laser or bubble-jet printer), of being able automatically to check your spelling and of having mistakes drawn to your attention. Sophisticated procedures like being able to personalize standard letters – even to the point of putting the appropriate name, address and greeting at the start – lie outside the scope of this book, but can save much time if used sensibly and cautiously.

The disadvantages apply to any form of computer-generated document. Just because whatever you write appears all neat and tidy on the screen, it may fool you into believing that it actually makes sense or is a good piece of writing. There is also the fact that it is, for some reason, extremely difficult to spot errors while looking for them on the screen. You usually have to print out a hard copy before you find all the mistakes, and this should become standard practice. You should *always* read through a hard copy of a document that has been produced on a word-processor. Again, a few corrections made by hand will indicate to the reader that you have taken trouble with your letter. Too many hand-made corrections, though, are a bad thing.

Handwritten letters and notes

If letters are superior to phone calls for certain types of communication, so handwritten letters are superior to anything more mechanically produced when the personal touch is of paramount importance. I would go so far as to say that if the these letters are not handwritten, then they should not be sent at all.

I will now begin to provide specimen letters. In some cases they are completely invented, in others – like the first – they derive from actual letters that I have received, or sent, myself.

SPECIMEN LETTER 1: HANDWRITTEN NOTE OF APOLOGY

PETER PAUL
Denman's Farm
Little Pottering
Brottesham
Northamptonshire
NN1 2XD

Telephone 0X23-31X53

24th April 199–

My dear John and Celia,

Horrors!! I completely forgot your party! I've just been clearing up the house (including the mantelpiece, where I've been throwing out all the invitations, which were starting to clog it up) and found your card beneath.

Infuriating, and rude.

Infuriating, also for me because I didn't do anything at all last night except have a row with Diana!

I *am* sorry.

Many apologies.

Oh God.

Oh dear.

Oh.
Love,

Peter

This is an almost completely successful attempt at making amends. The fact that Peter admits to having had a miserable time (and a row) convinces you of his sincerity. And yet it is done with a light touch. There is possibly a slightly unwelcome tone of bragging when he says that invitations were 'clogging up' his mantelpiece but that is not as far-fetched as a letter of apology I once received about a similar party 'no show'. The invitation was said to have become 'mixed up with the condolence letters for my wife's father who unfortunately died shortly before we received your kind invitation'. This, though possibly true, did not convince as it seemed to be trying to convince through introducing an irrelevant circumstance.

Unfortunately, Peter reduced the effectiveness of his note above by about 35 per cent, if not more. He wrote it on office notepaper . . .

SPECIMEN LETTER 2: HANDWRITTEN NOTE IN REPLY TO ONE ANNOUNCING A FORTHCOMING WEDDING

Flat 89
Barker Buildings
Lorraine Road
Manchester
MX1 5TG

Tel. 061-5X3 3444

1 May 199–

Dear Tim,

Great news! Your senses are no doubt so greatly inflamed with passion that you'll scarcely be able to read this scribble – but anyway MANY CONGRATULATIONS at flinging yourself headlong into a 'head over heels in love throw caution to the winds let's go ahead and to hell with the consequences anyway romance situation' (ongoing variety).

Both Helen and I are highly impatient to meet this talented and obviously forceful lady who has entwined her fingers so inexorably into your heartstrings in a very short space of time indeed! We in fact celebrated our *eighth* wedding anniversary this month and my penchant for satire immediately prompted me to offer you the advice 'The first eight years are the worst'. However Helen has censored that and insists on the following ammendment. ERRATUM: 'For worst read BEST in last line'.

Look forward to seeing you soon.

All our love,

Richard & Helen

Congratulators should also throw caution to the winds. This is not the time for a circumspect 'it won't last' approach. Open-hearted (if a bit hearty), good-humoured (if a mite clichéd at the end), this will do very nicely. What a pity that, in real life, Richard and Helen didn't actually stick it out much beyond their eight years, whereas Tim and his intended did . . .

 SPECIMEN LETTER 3: HANDWRITTEN LETTER OF CONGRATULATION

St Richard's Cottage
Corinthian Gardens
Marshland
Avon
BS3 8JR

Tel. 055X-547889

10 June 199–

Dear Stephen,

Very many congratulations on your new appointment. I look forward to hearing of further triumphs in the years to come.

I am enjoying immensely my retirement from 'that noblest of professions, sorriest of trades' and vegetating nobly under the shadow of the Mendips.

Best wishes for your future success,

Denis Robinson

A thankfully brief but effective note from a retired schoolmaster to a former pupil. On a strict word count the congratulator has more to say about himself than the congratulatee, but not so you would notice. The quotation is very schoolmasterly (I have no idea where it comes from . . .) but why not?

SPECIMEN LETTER 4: HANDWRITTEN POSTCARD
ACCEPTING AN APOLOGY FOR NON-ATTENDANCE

Canon T.A. Lawrence, The Cloisters, Farnham, Surrey, FA9 2SW
Tel. 098X-4555532

Thanks for your card. Delighted to hear of the event on 8th December. Of course you have every right to claim exemption – see St Luke Ch.14: v.20.

Blessings and good wishes.

T.A.L.

The biblical reference is a delightful tease: it states, 'And another said, I have married a wife, and therefore I cannot come.' That completely removes from the receiver of his message any suggestion that 'T.A.L.' was too disappointed at the invitation refusal.

Incidentally, I was once told that to write 'thanks for' instead of 'thank you for' was bad form. You may think this point the essence of gentility but, unfortunately, I have never been able to forget it.

2

PEN TO PAPER

The letters that you send are an expression of your personality. To put it rather grandly, they signify to the world how you wish to be considered, and they do this even before you have finished the first sentence. The paper and the printed address may get you off on the wrong foot even before you have written the first word.

Not that this should be a reason for nervousness on the writer's part. There is real pleasure and satisfaction to be gained from writing a letter that is not only well expressed, well presented and legible, but also looks good and feels good.

Give us the tools

When it comes to choosing writing materials, it is best to avoid:

- paper that is too thin (thickness is *not* a luxury)
- coloured paper
- lined paper (cranks use it)
- 'borrowed' hotel or office notepaper
- personalized paper that has cute little designs, pictures or logos on it
- stick-on labels in place of printed-on addresses. If you have neither, it may seem an imposition to have to write out your address every time, in full, but are you trying to impress, or not?
- inks other than navy blue or black (cranks use a different colour on alternate lines)
- biro, ball-point or felt-tip (for personal correspondence, at any rate)
- envelopes that are brown (except for business purposes)
- envelopes that have been put through the office franking machine

None of the above rejected options is entirely sinful, or plain wrong in itself, but each is questionable if you want to put over a favourable image of yourself. The degree of sinfulness in each case is, of course, debatable.

'Evil communications corrupt good manners.' – *1 Corinthians, 15:33*

'Remember that Charles Kingsley once received a letter from Dean Stanley, the illegibility of whose hand was notorious, at a time when Mrs Kingsley lay very ill. Kingsley examined the letter for many minutes in vain. At last he said: "I have every reason to believe this is a very kind letter of sympathy from Stanley – I feel sure it is. Yet the only two words I can even guess at are 'heartless devil'. But I pause – I pause to accept that suggestion as a likely one under the circumstances".' – quoted in *The Week-End Book* (1955)

As the materials in the letter writer's tool-kit are of the utmost importance – and as the exclusions listed earlier may have caused puzzlement – let us look at them one by one.

Stationery

Good thick notepaper and envelopes are delicious things to receive and handle and, yes, to keep. The plainness and simplicity of your writing materials speaks volumes. Who would ever wish to treasure a limp fax sheet, whatever information it contained? So, paper should be of a good thickness. Nothing is worse than flimsy paper that you can almost see through or which tears easily. Thickness is not a luxury, it gets your letter off to a good start, so go for as much of it as you can afford or as your political beliefs will allow. Bear in mind that recycled paper, although kind to the environment, usually looks as though it could do with a good wash. The recipient of your letter may not be as impressed with this as you are.

When it comes to choosing the size of your notepaper, consider whether you customarily write in a cramped little hand or in a vivacious scrawl, full of curls and flourishes. It is obvious that the latter handwriting will more quickly fill a sheet than the former. There is nothing more foolish than a tiny island of text floating in a vast ocean of unused paper. The solution, if you can run to it, is to have more than one size of notepaper so that you can choose the most appropriate for the occasion.

At one time it was not thought to be the done thing to have your address and telephone number printed on personal notepaper.

Engraved, handwritten, or applied by yourself with an embosser, yes, but not printed. There was no reason for this example of etiquette's artificial rule-making, though I suspect it was thought to smack of trade. The prohibition no longer applies. Unfortunately, nowadays, people have perhaps gone too far in the other extreme. They have become a little *too creative* with their personal printed notepaper, almost producing for themselves the equivalent of a personal logo in coats of many colours. A certain starkness is rather to be favoured. Black ink on good, white paper is still the best.

As to paper colour, there is nothing better than white or cream. Think very hard before going for anything else, whether it be grey or blue or any other shade. Consider not only what the colour will say about you but whether it will help the receiver actually read your letter. Dark blue ink on dark blue paper is, well, it's obvious really.

Lined paper should never be used (cranks use it, too). If you find it difficult writing on a straight line, use a ruled backing sheet.

It is naff to use the notepaper supplied by hotels other than for letters written while you are actually staying at the hotel. Otherwise, it will be quite obvious that you are too mean to use your own – and foolish enough to advertise the hotels that you have stayed in recently. Rather depends on how many stars they have, I suppose . . .

These days it is quite in order to write on both sides of a piece of notepaper, especially for a personal message. A more businessy letter writer would put the second page – or further pages – on continuation sheets (unheaded). I am always rather bemused when receiving letters which run on to a dozen or more sheets, particularly when the sheets are of small size. Am I supposed to be impressed? If so, I would reply that I would rather not be encouraged to judge the worth of a letter by its bulk – or weight.

When you have written the letter, it is best to choose an envelope which does not require your notepaper to be folded over too many times. Too many folds detracts from the impact of your letter. Unfolded paper gives the clearest look of all.

Letterheads

When it comes to these (i.e. pre-printed addresses on notepaper), again, the simplest and clearest designs are the best. Engraving is all very well, if you want to be that grand, but a simple black-on-white presentation of your address and telephone number is just as good. I have a particular antipathy to the use of italic type on letterheads, chiefly because it can be extremely difficult to work out what numbers and letters are trying to break out of the postal code.

For personal correspondence, the address should be centred:

The Larches
23, Railway Cuttings
Buckingham
Buckinghamshire
BU1 2ZF

Telephone 0X999 345671

Or it could be positioned over on the right, with the telephone number detached and placed elsewhere:

Telephone (0X999) 345671   The Larches
                                  23, Railway Cuttings
                                  Buckingham
                                  Buckinghamshire
                                  BU1 2ZF

Once upon a time, people living in the country would give details of the nearest railway station on a letterhead, but there is not much point in that now. Telephone numbers are not what they were either. When you could put 'MAYfair 1234' or 'JUNiper 2528' (in London) or (if you were an Earl of Home in Scotland) 'Coldstream 1', it was a much more distinctive thing than today's plain, scientific string of numbers.

It is always useful to put the dialling code, but there may be advantage in separating it from the actual phone number with a dash or by putting it within brackets.

There is no end to the variations that can be made on layout. But as for greater personalization on notepaper – the pre-printing of monograms, crests, coronets, logos and motifs – that is probably best avoided, unless there is very good reason for it. If you are not careful, such decorations can make personal notepaper seem like a trade calling card.

On the other hand, placing your name at the top of the notepaper is very helpful in that your recipient is in absolutely no doubt as to who is writing the letter. It also enables you to have a completely indecipherable signature and permits greater informality in the way you sign your name – possibly just your first name or initials – down below. Placing a name on notepaper would at one time have seemed a bit too much like 'trade' to be acceptable, but this no longer applies:

RICHARD THOMPSON	The Barn
	Needwell
	Branston
	Somerset
	TA23 7PQ
	Tel: 077X-333777
	Fax: 077X-777333

Reticence in the information given on your letterhead is no bad thing. I have seen letters from people in the public eye which merely have the name of the person at the top of the sheet, no address and certainly no telephone number. This preserves their privacy and makes it abundantly clear that they do not wish to enter into a long correspondence with the recipient. Quite a few show business people do this. Kenneth Williams had notepaper which simply had 'From: KENNETH WILLIAMS' at the top, nothing else at all.

Thirty years ago I received a letter from David Frost (to whom I had written asking him to speak at a meeting) which boldly displayed *my* address and the date in such a way that I had to look twice before seeing that David Frost had not put his own address. Very much depending on circumstances, there could be an argument for adopting this approach if you do wish to keep yourself to yourself.

Whatever formula you settle for, it will naturally be the case that when you have taken delivery of five hundred sheets of personalized notepaper and matching envelopes, you will then instantly find reason to move house.

Address labels

Using small, pre-printed, stick-on address labels is so widespread a practice as almost to be not worth complaining about, but it only shows that the user is not prepared to pay for printed notepaper or is not prepared to write the address on by hand. Little stickers with your address and phone number (even your surname) on may save you a lot of time if you don't wish to run to letterheads, but they are not very smart. Nor, for anything but the most basic communications, will letterheads do that you have cooked up for yourself on a word processor or with a John Bull printing outfit. Treat yourself to the real thing.

To put the name of a house within inverted commas, e.g. 'Dunroamin', is still considered incorrect and not the 'done thing'. More to the point, it is also unnecessary.

Indeed, on a general stylistic point, anyone who 'writes' with too frequent 'use' of 'inverted commas', if you 'know what I mean', is to be discouraged, if not referred for a medical opinion. As for people (!) who never miss an opportunity to put in exclamation marks (!!) , well, frankly, words fail me (!!!!)

Phone numbers

I have a version of my personal notepaper which does not give my telephone number. I can always add it on by hand if necessary, of course. It is not so much that I don't want any Tom, Dick and Harry to be able to ring me up, as that I want to make it impossible for people to ring me up trying to *sell* me things.

So, it is not just people with ex-directory telephone numbers who might do well to consider leaving their numbers off their notepaper – or even of having two sets of notepaper, one with, one without. Telephone selling – cold-calling, or what you will – is rampant and you may like to ensure that as many people as possible have to write to you instead of calling you up out of the blue.

Pleasing Mr Postman

Envelopes should be chosen, broadly speaking, to accompany (and match) your notepaper. White is smarter than brown. Envelopes that are brown should only be used for business purposes, paying bills and so on. There is a practical reason for this: it is less possible to detect a cheque or other pilferable enclosure if a brown envelope is held up to the light. 'Post office preferred' is a phrase that has arisen to describe envelopes that supposedly suit the criteria of size and shape decreed by the Post Office.

Envelopes that have been put through the office franking machine – to save you the postage – will also be viewed with suspicion by the recipient, as also envelopes with your employer's name printed on when you are writing a personal letter. Should envelopes be printed with your address and/or name on them? I think not. Leave that to tradespersons.

As for putting the sender's address on the envelope, for returning purposes if undelivered, this is universal practice when sending mail overseas but is not common for domestic mail (see, however, 'Mislaid in the mails', page 43). Should you not wish the Post Office to have to open your letter in order to return it to you, then putting an address on the back flap is essential.

The pen is mightier than the biro

After a period in which everyone seemed to fall for ball-points, felt-tipped or roller-ball pens, fountain pens are apparently now making a comeback. They are so much more pleasant to write with and (as with up-market motors cars and wrist watches), there is an individuality conferred on the user. You certainly don't get individuality with a biro.

More than one person has said to me that, since buying a proper fountain pen once again, they have found themselves writing *more* letters by hand and, indeed, writing more letters, period. The experience is just so enjoyable. So it might be that if you are suffering from writer's block, expenditure on a new pen might be the equivalent of a visit from Dyno-Rod.

Inks

To use inks other than navy blue or black might well serve to undo all the good work you are doing through writing your letters by hand – indeed, through sending letters at all. Cranks use a different colour on alternate lines, with special reference to red and green. To use an odd colour is the first step towards joining them.

Enough then of the letter writer's tool-kit. Now it is time to look at some more general matters that apply to all types of letter writing and are well worth pondering before putting pen to paper.

The right name

It is terribly important to spell the name of your letter's addressee correctly. Few of us are able to read a letter with a completely benign heart if it has begun by addressing us erroneously. For some reason people will always go for the least obvious spelling first. My own name

'Rees' is hardly difficult or uncommon, but most people plump for 'Reece'. Americans inevitably go for 'Reese' (as that is the commonest spelling of the name in the US) and an extraordinary number of others put the quasi-phonetic 'Reis'. My middle initial is T, so I have also received letters addressed to 'Mr N. Trees'.

I'll say it again: getting the name right is of the utmost importance. If you make a mistake writing or typing it, start again with a fresh piece of paper or a new envelope. If you don't know what the correct spelling is, try checking with the phone book. If it's really important, you might even have to phone up and find out. Above all, anticipate trouble. Is it 'Carole' with an 'e' or without? Is it 'Catherine', 'Katherine' or 'Katharine'? Is it 'Steven' or 'Stephen'? What's in a name? Rather a lot, actually.

Card sharp

There is absolutely no need to use notepaper if what you want to express can comfortably be accommodated on a postcard. A picture postcard might also be a pleasant thing to send (and it is worth remembering that if you put a picture postcard within an envelope you will probably be able to get more words on it, by using the address space).

Many people also use (plain – no picture) correspondence cards that are pre-printed across the top with their address, phone number, name or some combination of these three. These are extremely useful and can be used to avoid worrying how to address the recipient ('Dear Mike', 'Dear Mr . . .') because you can just plunge in with the message and squiggle your own initials or first name at the end of it.

For example:

Mrs Jack Spratt, 46, Tremilow Borings, Cheam, Surrey RG1 2TX
Tel. 09X9-356781

Or the word 'from' can be inserted:

From Lady Spratt, 78, Marmaduke Street, London WC1 2XY
Tel. 071-111 1111

Writing on both sides of a blank postcard can give you space for quite a long message but again without the need to be in any way formal.

Whatever type of postcard is chosen, it should still be placed in an envelope – if you want to do the thing properly. I suppose the reason for this is that a personal message, however innocuous, placed on an open postcard is rather public.

Personal matters

You should never hesitate to mark envelopes 'Personal and Confidential', even though you may risk alarming the recipient or raising his or her expectations. If the matter of the letter is for the receiver's eyes only, this is the only way to achieve that condition – though whether it will enable you to get your letter past some grand person's secretary or other minion is impossible to guarantee. The fact that in recent years letter-bombs have been marked 'Personal' means that caution has to be exercised with mail so labelled.

From post to pillar (overall layout)

What should the overall layout of a letter be? Traditionally, following the sender's address and the date of the letter has come the recipient's name and address, but it would seem unnecessary and a trifle grand to put the recipient's name and address at the top of a personal letter, or even at the top of a semi-informal one. This said, I admit very much to liking the style (common in the seventeenth and eighteenth centuries) of putting 'To [name of correspondent]' at the top of the letter, or '[name of correspondent with title]' at the close. Here, from the 'Letter Book of William Blundell the Cavalier' is the shape of a letter to his grandson (whom he rather oddly addresses as 'Nephew', a now obsolete term for grandson):

> *To my Grandson Nicholas*
> *London July 7th. 1686*
>
> *Nephew*
> *I have yours of June 28th which, as to the sense thereof I find to be humble and loving but I am sorry to perceive that the characters of your letters do still grow worse and worse. I may say the same of your spelling and of your leaving out of words. . . . And so with my blessing and daily prayers for your welfare, I will ever remain*
> *Your truly loving Grandfather.*

And here is that self-same Nicholas, now grown up and a Lancashire
squire, but with interesting spelling, writing in *his* letter book (1702-31) a
semi-formal notification of his father's death:

> *To Mr Joseph Hawley at Martin Sands*
> *August the 13th 1702*
>
> *Yours Mr Hawley of the 8th Ultimo came not to hand till the tenth*
> *currant . . . . I wish it had so pleased God to order it otherwayes but the*
> *Almighty has thought fit to take my Dearest Father out of this world*
> *to a better . . . . I am beholding to your for your troble, you having don*
> *all you were desired in it by which you have oblidged your Servant.*
> *Nicho. Blundell*

The second of these notes also demonstrates how useful this method
could be nowadays when you aren't sure how familiarly to address
your correspondent, or whether to put 'Miss, Mrs, Ms' at the start. You
could just plunge straight into the letter (rather as you might do
nowadays on a postcard).

The other method is simply to put the name of the recipient at the *end*
of the letter, usually with title; in the above case this would have been
'Joseph Hawley, Esq.'. I would dearly like to see this method reintro-
duced, though probably without the title, just the name. To show you
what I mean, here is a brief note written in longhand by Matthew
Arnold (1822-88), obviously replying to someone who had written to
express an opinion:

Dear Sir,

Actual Catholicism I think a lost cause, but I quite agree that a
renewed and transformed Catholicism may have a great future
before it – and not among the Celtic races only.

Faithfully yours,

Matthew Arnold

Rev. John Oliver

(This also strikes me as being admirably to the point – and civil –
without sparing the Revd. Oliver a word more than he deserves.)

Post-worthy

What should the construction of a letter be from the point of view of content? A personal letter whose aim is simply to keep in touch will probably be as formless as conversation usually is. About the only rule I would insist on is that very early in the letter you should make it plain whether you are replying to an earlier letter or writing off your own bat. If responding, then for heaven's sake react to the letter you have received and show that you have in fact received it. Begin by acknowledging your correspondent's letter specifically (even by mentioning its date) – to show that you have received it and are not just writing out of the blue. This helps allay worries that letters have been mislaid or have crossed in the post. This informs your correspondent that you did indeed receive that earlier letter. If so, respond to any points that your correspondent has made and answer any questions. It is infuriating when correspondents do not appear to have registered what you have written to them. *A golden rule when replying to a letter is to have it in front of you when you are composing the reply.*

If a personal letter has a particular purpose – to thank, congratulate, condole, or whatever – then a similar basic rule operates as with non-private correspondence: you should make it plain in the first paragraph, if not the first sentence, *what the letter is about*. Then set out your material as naturally and logically as possible. Use short sentences and short paragraphs whenever you are able.

If you are attempting something difficult, whether that is setting down a complex argument or expressing some emotional complication, it makes obvious sense to *draft* your letter. Once upon a time, in the days of letter books and before the advent of carbon paper and other copying methods, this was common practice. The draft meant that you produced a fairer copy of the letter to send, and also that you had a copy to keep for yourself. Drafting now seems rather a burden but word processors can usefully be employed here to produce an impeccable text when the occasion justifies it.

The most important things to remember regarding letter-writing style are:

- *Try not to impress the person you are writing to*. Be yourself.
- *Try to reproduce yourself as you write*. Write as you speak, but not as though you are making a speech.

I have just received a letter which begins 'May I take this opportunity' and continues 'I am not acquainted with . . .' The first phrase sounds like a Lord Mayor revving up for a speech, the second was good old periphrasis; why not say, 'I don't know . . .'?

In Victorian times Lord Clarendon told Louisa, Duchess of Manchester (and later Duchess of Devonshire): 'The charm of a letter is to be like the conversation of the writer and that is just what your letters are.' That is a great compliment. There is a difference between a letter which reproduces someone's spoken charms and what is often referred to as a 'chatty' letter. The latter kind is only producible by a certain type of person – the type who is only capable of producing three pages where one paragraph would do. I think they have actually been encouraged to write like this, at an early age, but it appears difficult to eradicate the madness. They have to give you all kinds of secondary detail, they cannot get quickly to the point, and because their punctuation is often non-existent, there is really no stopping them. If only they could think in terms of short sentences, it might just reduce their tendency to rattle on.

Indeed, *brevity* is the soul of letter writing, or should be. There are some people who cannot be brief when writing, just as there are people who lose all track of time when making a speech. There is no excuse for this, except that, as several people have said, it is more troublesome to be brief than it is to be long-winded. But there is no virtue in writing screeds, although some people seem to think that there is value in volume. Why else, for example, do they write large and send you a sackful of sheets when, sensibly sized, the same number of words would fit on one sheet or two?

The days of long-letter writing belong to the relaxed era of the long novel. Correspondence was intended to keep sender and receiver occupied, to fill in time. Nowadays, writing a long letter may make the sender happy but will not, in most cases, be welcomed by the recipient. Always ask yourself whether a full-blown letter might not be more effective as a short one. And then remember the famous exchange of notes between the Prince de Joinville and the French actress Rachel (who died in 1858). He wrote, 'Where? When? How much?' She replied, 'Your place. Tonight. Free.' The resulting affair lasted seven or eight years.

'*Verbosa et grandis epistula venit/A Capreis*' ('A huge and wordy letter came from Capri'). – Juvenal, *Satires*, x.71 (*c.* 100 – *c.* 128)

'The letter is too long by half a mile.' – William Shakespeare, *Love's Labour's Lost*, V.ii.54 (1592-3)

'All letters, methinks, should be as free and easy as one's discourse, not studied as an oration, nor made up of hard words like a charm.' – Dorothy Osborne (Lady Temple), in a letter to Sir William Temple (October 1653)

'I have made this a rather long letter because I haven't had time to make it shorter.' – Blaise Pascal (1623-62), *Pensées, The Provincial Letters*, xvi (1657)

'A short letter to a distant friend is, in my opinion, an insult like that of a slight bow or cursory salutation; a proof of unwillingness to do much, even where there is a necessity of doing something.' – Samuel Johnson, Letter to Joseph Baretti (10 June 1761)

'Essays that act the part of letters are mighty insipid things, and when one has nothing occasional to say, it is better to say nothing.' – Horace Walpole, Letter to Mary Berry (18 September 1789)

'"That's rather a sudden pull up, ain't it, Sammy?" inquired Mr Weller. "Not a bit on it," said Sam; she'll vish there was more, and that's the great art o' letter writin'".' – Charles Dickens, *Pickwick Papers*, Chap. 33 (1836-7)

'I am going to write to you . . . but not now, for I haven't anything to do and I can't write letters except when I am rushed.' – Mark Twain (1835-1910)

Be brief in your choice of words also. *Long words* obtrude in a personal letter and can make it sound pompous. *Jargon* is also to be avoided, obviously when writing to someone who may not understand it, but even to someone who does. Avoid *clichés* like the plague – as someone once said. There is a natural temptation to rely on off-the-peg phrases; they come to us without our having to think about them and they do indeed provide an easy way of exchanging recognition between correspondents. But they should be drummed out, for the most part. They are not hard to spot – that's the whole point; they are mind-numbingly familiar:

- at the end of the day
- in the final analysis
- the moment of truth
- . . . is the name of the game
- alive and well and living in . . .
- only time will tell
- it will set alarm bells ringing
- like a dream come true
- over the moon
- a legend in her own lifetime

- I would like to apologize for any inconvenience that you may have been caused
- the rest is history
- when the chips are down
- journey into the unknown
- long, hot summer
- his death diminishes us all
- at this moment in time
- this day and age
- in point of fact

So, say what you have to say in *your own words* – simply and directly (and warmly). That will make you sound like a human being rather than an 'I speak your weight' machine.

Above all, *listen to what you are writing*. If it reads well out loud, it will probably read well off the page. An employee of the Royal Borough of Windsor and Maidenhead wrote to a householder in 1981 and asked him to trim a hedge. He did so in these words: 'Whereas a hedge situation at Altwood Road, Maidenhead in Berkshire, belonging to you overhangs the highway known as Altwood Road, Maidenhead aforesaid, so as to endanger or obstruct the passage of pedestrians. . . .' Need I quote more? (Oddly, as long ago as 22 August 1934, *The Times* was drawing attention to the trend: 'A popular dodge at present is to add the word "situation" or "position" to a noun; by this means, apparently, it has been discovered that the most pregnant meanings can be expressed with the least effort. The "coal situation" remains unchanged; the "herring position" is grave.') The point is that if the Windsor council employee had read his letter out loud he would, with a bit of luck, never have sent it. Even the most cloth-eared person is more likely to perceive the ludicrousness of the 'situation' additive if it reaches his brain through ear rather than eye.

Irony is to be handled with care. Some people and some nations (I am thinking of the US here) are almost incapable of appreciating irony or even of detecting it. Remember what Alan Bennett said about the use of irony. In his play *Forty Years On*, a character taking part in a parody of between-the-wars attitudes delivered the line: 'A divorced woman on the throne of the House of Windsor would be a pretty big feather in the cap of that bunch of rootless intellectuals, alien Jews and international pederasts who call themselves the Labour Party.' Bennett claimed to have heard people in the audience saying 'Hear, hear', taking the line at face value. He concluded that if you are going to be ironic you should be preceded by a man waving a red flag.

This is another way of saying that *clarity* is important if you are going to achieve your intention in writing any letter. The use of bright phrases can, in fact, tend to obscure your meaning every bit as much as the use of jargon and clichés. I once lost a considerable amount of money because, when discussing in a letter the clauses in a contract, I said, 'I think we had better wave that one through'. What I meant was, 'agree to it without argument', but the receiver of my letter thought I meant 'waive it', i.e. give in. A cautionary tale.

Possibly that misfortune befell me because my correspondent thought I was making a pun. It is a very good rule to avoid *puns* if at all possible (especially if you feel obliged to add 'no pun intended!' or 'if you'll excuse the pun!!' in brackets afterwards.) There are some people who are compulsive punsters in writing just as much as in speech. They should have our sympathy but should not be encouraged. There is no such thing as a good pun (though there are occasionally clever ones) and generally they sound like jokes going off at half-cock. They are to letter writing what watering the beer is to brewing.

How important are *grammar, punctuation and spelling*? There is a sense in which these things don't matter. In a personal handwritten letter a mistake in grammar can be excused because it may not be quite clear what the writer intended. Besides, to split an infinitive is not yet a capital offence, though there are people who would like it to be so. And again, if there is an error in a business letter, perhaps it was because the secretary made it (though the originator of the letter ought to have checked the finished item and winkled it out before posting).

But anything which detracts from a letter – and anything which *distracts* the reader from understanding and appreciating a letter – is obviously a bad thing. A story is told of Georges Courteline (*d.* 1929), the French playwright and humorous writer, who received a letter of complaint from a lesser and younger writer in pursuit of publicity. The younger man demanded satisfaction for some imagined insult but employed atrocious spelling and illegible handwriting. Courteline replied: 'My dear young sir: As I am the offended party, the choice of weapons is mine. We shall fight with orthography. And you are already dead!'

The actor Peter Sellers once received a fan letter which read: 'Dear Mr Sellers, I have been a keen follower of yours for many years now, and should be most grateful if you would kindly send me a singed photograph of yourself.' Unable to ignore this unfortunate spelling mistake, Sellers took a photograph and burned it round the edges using a cigarette lighter. A few weeks later, another letter arrived from the fan thanking him for the photograph, but adding, 'I wonder if I could trouble you for another as this one is signed all round the edge.' Now, I must confess to being uncertain in many areas of grammar myself. Is it 'will' or 'shall', 'would' or 'should'? I could have the distinctions explained to me till doomsday and I would (or should) not be able to grasp them. So when I come to one of these testing points – I quite often recast the sentence and find another way of saying what I have to say. Cowardly, maybe, but pragmatic.

The point is that if there is no logic to your punctuation, if you put apostrophes in the wrong place (I get letters from one source addressed to 'Nigel Ree's' – honestly) or nowhere at all ('Its been a terrible week'), if you continue to regularly split infinitives, and if you confuse singular and plural entities ('The Government cannot make their mind up'), of if you make obvious spelling misteaks, it will get in the way of your message. It will distract the attention of the reader from what you have to say. A little attention to detail, the occasional trip to the dictionary, a general simplicity of approach, will help you produce readable letters.

'As our alphabet now stands, the bad spelling, or what is called so, is generally the best, as conforming to the sound of the letters and of the words.' – Benjamin Franklin (1786)

'A man occupied with public or other important business cannot, and need not, attend to spelling.' – Napoleon I (1769-1821)

'Do you spell it with a "V" or a "W"?' inquired the judge. 'That depends upon the taste and fancy of the speller, my Lord,' replied Sam (Weller). – Charles Dickens, *Pickwick Papers* (1836-7)

'The spelling of words is subordinate. Morbidness for nice spelling and tenacity for or against some one letter or so means dandyism and impotence in literature.' – Walt Whitman (1856)

'It is a pity that Chawcer, who had geneyus, was so unedicated; he's the wuss speller I know of.' – 'Artemus Ward' (C.F. Browne) (c. 1867)

'They spell it Vinci and pronounce it Vinchy; foreigners always spell better than they pronounce.' – Mark Twain, *The Innocents Abroad* (1869)

'I don't see any use in spelling a word right, and never did. I mean I don't see any use in having a uniform and arbitrary way of spelling words. We might as well make all our clothes alike and cook all dishes alike.' – Mark Twain (1875)

> 'I don't give a damn for a man that can spell a word only one way.' – Mark Twain

> 'Who cares about spelling? Milton spelt *dog* with two *g*'s. The American Milton, when he comes, may spell it with three, while all the world wonders, if he is so minded.' – Augustine Birrell (1894)

> 'She even makes mistakes in spelling, and in my opinion that's essential in a woman.' – Auguste Renoir (*d.* 1919)

> 'My spelling is Wobbly. It's good spelling but it Wobbles, and letters get in the wrong places.' – A.A. Milne, *Winnie-the-Pooh*, Chap. 6 (1926)

The trouble with my laying down the law on stylistic points and my recommending that you do or don't do certain things is that your letters could become dry, cautious, inoffensive documents which singularly fail to express your thoughts and personality in your own distinctive way. For example, I am tempted to say, 'Don't put in too much *underlining*' – in addition to the exclamation marks, already warned against – 'and don't make use of EXCESSIVE CAPITALIZATION.' I mean, Queen Victoria was manic in this respect:

> I *never* NEVER spent such an evening!! My *dearest DEAREST DEAR* Albert sat on a footstool by my side. . . . How can I ever be thankful enough to have such a *Husband*!

But, on the other hand, if she hadn't gone so far over the top doing this, her letters would have been rather boring and they certainly would not have been distinctively hers.

A final, small stylistic point. Somewhere or other along life's path I was told – I think it was by my mother, actually – that you should *never begin a letter with the word 'I'*. Naturally, I frequently break this rule but you can see there is a certain point to it. A letter with every paragraph starting with 'I' would look more like a manifesto than a friendly letter. Here is part of one I received recently from my bank manager:

Dear Mr Rees

I have recently replaced —— ——, previous Manager of this branch who has left to assume duties elsewhere within the bank.

Following a review of your accounts, I note that . . .

I hope that you will be able to take advantage of this opportunity
which will, at the very least, give you reassurance that your affairs
have been reviewed professionally . . .

I am able to confirm that no charge will be made for this interview
and that you are under no obligation to act on the advice given.

I look forward to hearing from you.

I think my mother had a point.

The mail coach

The foregoing is designed to show how the letter writer, by taking care
over certain aspects of the craft, may be of help to the letter reader who
is on the receiving end of any epistle. How else can you be a model
correspondent?

Put the *date* on your letters. No, this is not because you expect your
correspondence to be published one day or because it will be useful for
purposes of the historical record. It is useful in the here and now. But it
is surprising how often letters are not dated, leading to all kinds of
confusion. If I receive an undated letter, I scribble on it the date I
receive it.

Mention *enclosures* in the letter – don't just let them wash around in
the envelope. They may subsequently get separated from your letter
and it may be important for you to have a note of what accompanied the
letter.

Keep track of your correspondence with a *letter book*. By this, I mean a
book which records when you post off particular letters, especially those
which require an answer. This enables you to chase up unanswered
letters more efficiently and easily. It also provides you with a record of
when, say, tax payments were posted off.

Now this may sound a very arduous process – almost as unlikely to
be kept going for very long as a diary – but I have known several people
who have maintained letter books in our century and it undoubtedly
gives great peace of mind, if only to people with orderly minds. The
original meaning of the term 'letter book' was slightly different,
however. One that I know about is that kept by Nicholas Blundell, a

Lancashire squire, between 1702 and 1731 (and mentioned in *The Great Diurnall of Nicholas Blundell*, 3 vols., published by the Record Society of Lancashire and Cheshire, 1968-72). Blundell's book contained first drafts and rough copies of letters which he would then write 'fair over' for his correspondents. Today, of course, it provides a useful historical record, but in Nicholas Blundell's day it was the equivalent of carbon paper and photocopying. It must have been laborious, all that writing out and rewriting letters (great men had people to do it for them, of course), but it can only have made for more considered and better constructed letters.

Keeping copies

To keep copies of the personal letters that you send assumes either self-importance on your part or simple good sense. Depending on the circumstances, there could be very good reason to keep a record of precisely what you wrote on some personal matter, just as it is perfectly sensible to keep records of what you write on business and professional issues. Making copies these days is hardly a difficult matter. After a period of time has elapsed and you are convinced that the copy is no longer of importance, you can have a weeding-out session to keep your files reasonably slim.

Keeping envelopes

In professional environments it is quite normal practice to clip the envelope to the letter as soon as it is opened. The point of this is to ensure that any details of posting date, address of addressee and sender, and so on are retained in case they are not obvious from the letter.

'We lay aside letters never to read them again, and at last we destroy them out of discretion, and so disappears the most beautiful, the most immediate breath of life, irrecoverably for ourselves and for others.' – Goethe, *Elective Affinities* (1809)

'And I copied all the letters in a big round hand/[and] . . . now I am the Ruler of the Queen's Navee!' – W.S. Gilbert, *HMS Pinafore*, Act I (1878)

'Never burn an uninteresting letter is the first rule of British aristocracy.' – Frank Moore Colby (1865-1925)

'Letters are like wine: if they are sound they ripen with keeping. A man should lay down letters as he does a cellar of wine.' – Samuel Butler, *Notebooks* (c 1890).

'Sydney Smith, or Napoleon or Marcus Aurelius (somebody about that time) said that after ten days any letter would answer itself. You see what he meant.' – A.A. Milne. (In fact, it was Arthur Binstead in *Pitcher's Proverbs* (1909), who said, 'The great secret in life . . . [is] not to open letters for a fortnight. At the expiration of that period you will find that nearly all of them have answered themselves.')

'Answered some/Of his long marvellous letters but kept none.' – W.H. Auden, in his poem 'Who's Who' (*c.* 1934)

Keeping letters

Yes, you should keep letters, for as long as it is practicable to do so. Reading – and handling – old letters is one of life's great pleasures. *Littera scripta manet*, as the old saying has it – 'the written letter remains'. Correspondence endures, unlike some pleasures, and advantage should be taken of the fact. On the other hand, throwing letters away – after a suitable period of time has elapsed – is almost as agreeable. Remember the story recounted by Margaret Truman, daughter of Harry S Truman. One day the American President found his wife, Bess, at the fireplace burning the letters he had written to her over the years. 'But think of history!' he protested. 'I *have*,' she replied.

Never write the kind of letters which ask the receivers to destroy them – they won't.

❦ 3 ❦

POSTMAN'S BLOCK

If you have read this far, you will either have been given some useful pointers which should enable you to write better letters, or you may have been reduced to a state of frozen incapacity by the rules and regulations I have so gently advanced. The latter won't do, of course, as the purpose of this book is to make letter writing easier.

So, what should you do if you continue to find letter writing difficult? How do you overcome 'postman's block' – a reluctance, an inability to put pen to paper? That is what this short chapter is about.

The chief thing to remind yourself is, in the words of a reasonably illustrious advertising campaign that the Post Office ran in the 1960s, that 'Someone Somewhere Wants a Letter from You'. We all, most of us anyway, actively *like* receiving letters, so if you write one the chances are that you will actually please the person to whom you address it. Surely that is as good a reason as any to overcome any reluctance you may have?

As with all forms of writing, however, there is a feeling, an almost physical obstacle to overcome before sitting down to pen a letter. Novelists have strange rituals before they get to work – ritually sharpening their pencils, putting on a favourite piece of music, screwing their feet to the floor in front of the desk, and so on – but writing a simple letter is not exactly like embarking on *War and Peace*, so come on!

From my own experience as a writer in the general sense I would pass on two helpful thoughts – talismans, if you like. One is, don't hang about waiting for inspiration to come. 'Start making marks on paper,' as someone rather helpfully put it. Curiously, by making marks, you bring about the creation of other marks. Writing anything has a way of facilitating writing something. This method may mean that you have to go back and revise what you have written – and you may not wish to get into the business of doing drafts and making fair copies – but it very definitely works.

Another way of putting this is, 'Start writing, write anything, write gibberish.' The novelist Katherine Mansfield put it yet a third way in her journal: 'Better far write twaddle or anything, anything, than nothing at all.' Out of the verbiage will come something useful. Believe me.

'You say there is nothing to write about. Then write to me that there is nothing to write about.' – Pliny the Younger (d. 113), *Letters*, I

'One of the pleasures of reading old letters is the knowledge that they need no answer.' – Lord Byron (d. 1824)

'Correspondences are like small-clothes before the invention of suspenders; it is impossible to keep them up.' – Revd Sydney Smith in a letter to Mrs Crowe (31 January 1841)

'Spanish dynasties come and go . . . but there is one thing in Spain that is always the same – they never answer letters.' – George Villiers, Earl of Clarendon, alleged remark (1846)

'An intention to write never turns into a letter. A letter must happen to one like a surprise, and one may not know where in the day there was room for it to come into being.' – Rainer Maria Rilke, *Letters 1892-1910*

'Due to unknown motives, Jones left a letter for several days on his desk, forgetting each time to post it. He ultimately posted it, but it was returned to him from the Dead-letter Office because he forgot to address it. After addressing it and posting it a second time, it was again returned to him, this time without a stamp. He was then forced to recognize the unconscious opposition to the sending of the letter.' – Sigmund Freud, *The Psychopathology of Everyday Life* (1904)

'Don't you like to write letters? I do because it's such a swell way to keep from working and yet you feel you've done something.' – Ernest Hemingway in a letter to F. Scott Fitzgerald (1925)

'Why it should be such an effort to write to the people one loves I can't imagine. It's none at all to write to those who don't really count.' – Katherine Mansfield, *Journals* (1954)

'The letter which merely answers another letter is no letter at all.' – Mark Van Doren, quoted by Clifton Fadiman in *Any Number Can Play* (1957)

'I would have answered your letter sooner, but you didn't send one.' – Goodman Ace in a letter (1950) to Groucho Marx, quoted in *The Groucho Letters* (1967)

By return of post

The most obvious prompt for you to write a letter is when you have already received one that needs replying to. In this situation another aid to overcoming postman's block is to have the original letter in front of you as you write (which I recommend anyway as normal practice). If necessary, copy out the points your correspondent has made and then methodically respond to each one.

But not all letters require replies. So when is a reply called for and when is it not? By and large this will be obvious. Either your correspondent will ask you questions which require answering or you will be able to detect whether they can be dealt with at another time and are simply being posed rhetorically. (See also 'Are replies really necessary?', Chapter 6, page 76.)

There are occasions when tactfully ignoring the demands or the points made by your correspondent is the most diplomatic thing to do. In 1962, during the Cuban Missiles Crisis, the Soviet leader, Nikita Khrushchev sent two letters to President Kennedy. The first was very threatening. No, he would not be withdrawing Soviet missiles from Cuba. The Americans must stop their blockade of Soviet shipping forthwith, or else Armageddon would ensue.

The second letter was much more conciliatory in tone and held open the possiblity of negotiation and compromise. The fact that the second letter had been sent hard on the heels of the first, without waiting for reply, was seen as indicating Khrushchev's volatile state of mind and his probable willingness to be more cooperative. In a text-book example of diplomatic wisdom, the Americans decided to ignore the first letter and reply only to the second . . .

When dealing with letters that make you very angry and which nothing will stop you from hurling back, just hold on a minute. The golden rule is to sleep on it before replying. That way there is more chance that you will reach a sensible decision as to whether it is really worth replying at all.

Abraham Lincoln once advised Edwin Stanton, his secretary of war, to put a letter in the stove rather than send it. 'That's what I do when I have written a letter while I am angry. It's a good letter and you had a good time writing it and feel better. Now, burn it and write another.'

According to Randolph Churchill's book *Lord Derby* (1960), the 17th Earl of Derby wrote a letter to the Foreign Secretary in 1919, beginning, 'My Dear Curzon, I have always known you to be a cad. I now know you to be a liar.' The letter did not go off in the night bag from the Paris Embassy, so the next morning Derby looked at it again. 'Hmmm. Perhaps it's a bit strong. I think I'll have another go.' This time the letter began, 'My Dear George, you and I have known each other too long to quarrel over so small a matter . . .'

Are you beginning to get the message?

'Letters written after dinner are read in Hell.' – Turkish proverb

'Never answer a letter when you are angry.' – Chinese proverb

'I pray you, in your letters,
When you shall these unlucky deeds relate,
Speak of me as I am; nothing extenuate,
Nor set down aught in malice.' – William Shakespeare, *Othello*, V.ii.341
(1604)

At these moments, as at all others, it should be remembered that letters have a permanence which could prove embarrassing to the sender, especially if they have been dashed off in the heat of the moment. Although a spoken remark could result in an action for slander, how much more likely it is that an injudicious comment written down in ink for all to see will one day, sooner not later, return to haunt the person who wrote it.

Wait a minute, Mr Postman

Pause before you post. Even if your letter has not been written in white-hot anger and is of a non-controversial nature, there is still good reason to wait a while before sealing the envelope and posting off.

Always re-read what you have written before sending. As I have already said, it is worth reading the letter aloud, too. If a letter reads well aloud, it will probably read well silently, too.

'Do not close a letter without reading it.' – American proverb

---

But do, please, write

There are few things worse than a dilatory correspondent. Manuel de Falla (1876-1946), the Spanish composer, was a notoriously reluctant letter writer and there would always be an enormous pile of unanswered mail sitting on his desk. When de Falla learned of the death of the painter Ignacio Zuloaga, he was much put out. 'What a shame!' he cried. 'He died before I could answer his letter – the one he sent me five years ago . . .'

There is no point in arguing that a *too prompt* response to a letter is somehow ungentlemanly or undiplomatic or just plain pushy. That won't wash any more. Thomas Jefferson may once have said of the US minister to Spain, 'I have not heard from him for two years. If I don't hear from him next year, I will have to write him a letter . . .' That was in another time when other manners prevailed.

So, no more prevarication. Write that letter *now*. After all, it is only a letter you need to write. It is not quite as hard as climbing Mount Everest.

If you still find it difficult writing letters, take heart from these views on the matter, both for and against:

'For his letters, say they, are weighty and powerful; but his bodily presence is weak, and his speech contemptible.' – Second Epistle to the Corinthians, 10:10

'It is generally better to deal by speech than by letter.' – Francis Bacon, *Essays*, No. 47, 'Of Negotiating' (1625)

'A letter is a deliberate and written conversation.' – Baltasar Gracián, *The Art of Worldly Wisdom*, cxlviii (1647)

'One glimpse of the human face, and shake of the human hand, is better than whole reams of this cold, thin correspondence; yea, of more than all the letters that have sweated the fingers of sensibility, from Madame Sévigné and Balzac to Sterne and Shenstone.' – Charles Lamb, Letter to Thomas Manning (9 August 1800)

'Oh, the glory, the freedom, the passion of a letter! It is worth all the lip-talk in the world.' – Donald G. Mitchell (Ik Marvel), *Reveries of a Bachelor* (1850)

'"Christ Almighty – another letter from my father!" said the Earl of Chesterfield's son.' – Caryl Brahms & S.J. Simon, *No Nightingale*, Chap. 15, 1944)

Of such is the importance of letters.

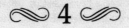

THE RIGHT ADDRESS

This chapter deals with two types of address: where a person lives (and how to show that on the envelope), plus how to write that person's name and title on the envelope and how to refer to that person in the letter.

If you do not think you have an accurate address for your correspondent, the first place to try is the phone book (which, not before time, is now getting round to giving post codes). If you want to find out or check a post code, all Post Offices have a booklet which you can refer to and which will enable you to pin down the correct code from the information contained in the rest of the address (anywhere in the country).

Other sources of addresses include Yellow Pages and other business directories. Phone companies will not usually give out an address if you simply proffer a name and telephone number. Companies or organizations are also, correctly, reluctant to give out over the phone private addresses of employees and others to any random caller. They will usually, however, undertake to redirect mail if it is addressed care of (c/o) the company or organization.

Addresses for people in the public eye or in public life – and whose phone numbers are likely to be ex-directory in any case – may sometimes be found in *Who's Who* and *Debrett's People of Today*. If not a private address, then a business address or that of a bank or of an agent will be given. In quite a large number of cases, however, no address is given at all. A letter sent to an actor's agent or to a politician c/o the House of Commons or the House of Lords will, in most cases, find its way to the right pigeon-hole or be forwarded.

It can sometimes be difficult to trace the head offices of commercial organizations or professional associations, as you may not know which phone book to look in. Most public libraries, however, will have copies of publications listing professional associations, sports and hobbies organizations, and specialist fan clubs. Often the best way of reaching a public figure is to write c/o a broadcasting organization or newspaper and they will forward your letter. It helps considerably if you can indicate clearly which programme you have seen the person on and, if possible, which company produced the programme. Just because you saw someone on TV in Aberdeen doesn't mean to say that the programme originated there . . .

If writing to someone who has contributed an article to a newspaper or magazine, it makes it easier for your letter to be forwarded if you put the date of the article and even the page on which it appeared.

One of these methods is sure to work. Putting 'Personal' or 'Private' *may* mean that the communication gets nearer to a public figure before being intercepted and dealt with by a minion, but it is no guarantee. As mentioned previously, security alertness these days for letter bombs and such means that very few people in public life still actually open their own mail.

The fact that letters can be forwarded or redirected free of charge is a small but unsung benefit of often-criticized postal services. It makes the tracking down of elusive prey so much easier.

The Post Office prefers . . .

How do you get your letter to the right address? The Post Office encourages the use of full addresses, including counties, even when a PO Box number is being used and even when there is a post code given. This is because not all sorting offices are capable of handling the post codes which, theoretically, contain all the information necessary to target a small delivery area (though not always the precise letter box).

I should think it might also have something to do with the fact that many people write the post codes illegibly – which would not have occurred to such a degree if an all-numbers zip-code system had been chosen, as in the United States. But that is by the by.

So, however tedious it may be, putting full addresses is the advisable thing to do. 'It makes it easier – and quicker – for us to sort your mail if you write the POST TOWN in capitals', the Post Office states in its 'Post Guide'. In addition, I prefer writing out the county name in full rather than use the traditional odd abbreviations – 'Herts' for 'Hertfordshire', 'Oxon' for 'Oxfordshire', 'Salop' for Shropshire, and so on. The post code should also be put on a separate line and *not* underlined.

Punctuation in addresses is a science in itself. I once worked for a company which instructed secretaries to omit *all* punctuation from addresses (and also from the body of letters – 'open' punctuation, I believe it is called). It was rumoured that this was to make a saving on the cost of typewriter ribbons. I agree with this up to a point as it can lead to a generally cleaner appearance, though a comma after a house number *can* make it clearer. Hence, what I would recommend is something like this:

Horace Gentleman
The Larches
22, Fortescue Road
TOWNSVILLE
Countyshire
AA1 XY2

Incidentally, although the Post Office has no view on the matter (as far as I can make out), putting the name of your house within inverted commas – e.g. 'Dunroamin' – is not the done thing in polite circles. It is also pretty naff (as is most putting of things 'within' inverted 'commas' – see page 19).

The name on the envelope

As I will say again before this chapter is out, I am of the school that believes in removing handles from names – if only for the reason that it lessens the need to agonize over what people would like, or ought, to be called, 'Mr' or 'Esq.', 'Mrs', 'Miss' or 'Ms'. So just as I find that 'Dear Nigel Rees' at the start of letter gets over *that* problem, so plain 'Nigel Rees' on the envelope removes any dithering over whether I would like to be 'Mr' or 'Esq.' or neither.

Similarly, putting on the envelope 'The Customer Services Manager, XYZ Corporation' and beginning the letter 'Dear Customer Services Manager' removes any need to speculate on the sex of the said person and avoids use of the unfriendly 'Dear Sir or Madam' approach.

You see, I would really rather not receive letters addressed to me as 'Nigel Rees, Esq.' That really does seem a pretty pointless form of address these days. I don't even particularly want to be addressed, in print, as 'Mr'. 'Mr Nigel Rees' signals to me that my correspondent has decided, of his own accord, that I am not up to 'Esq.' and am thus to be treated like a tradesman, but I know that others don't mind the Mr/Mrs/Miss/Ms form.

So, I would rather just be addressed by name alone, without any title whatever. Of course, it is easy for me to take this attitude within the easy familiarity of the media, but I wish other people would join me there. It would help to overcome all sorts of problems. If all such common or garden handles were abolished (I am not suggesting, though, that 'Sirs' and 'Lords' and 'Reverends' and military ranks should get the chop), there would be much less scope for contention or for offence to being taken.

Women's agonizing over whether to be 'Miss', 'Mrs' or 'Ms' would be finished at a stroke, if they just stuck to their names. You don't have to be a rabid feminist to appreciate that some women when they marry do not wish to submerge their identity in their husband's by becoming known as 'Mrs John Smith'. There is no legal requirement for them to do such a thing, anyway, though in the days (very recent) when the Inland Revenue maintained the prehistoric practice of dealing with the husband over his wife's tax affairs, it was impossible to refer to a wife solely by her unmarried name. 'Jane Golightly a.k.a. [also known as] Mrs J.P. Smith' would soon creep in.

How much more sensible is the American fashion for *adding on* the husband's name upon marriage (sometimes with a hyphen, sometimes not). This can give rise to some oddities, of which 'Arianna Stassinopoulos Huffington' is probably the oddest, but it makes what has happened perfectly clear. And then, should the worst happen, and the marriage fail, the husband's surname can simply be lopped off again. (Farrah Fawcett Majors, for example, went back to being Farrah Fawcett.) By contrast, how many women in British public life have found fame under their married names and then been condemned to keep them even after divorce? Alas, the American fashion will not seem to take on in Britain, it appears.

Another way of getting round this problem is – in semi-formal correspondence, anyway – to call a married woman by both name forms. This has the added advantage of making absolutely clear what her status is, as well as hinting that she is not too happy with people who misunderstand. Thus, 'Mrs David M. Married (Jessica Single)' or 'Jessica Single (Mrs David M. Married)' or (in the US) 'Jessica Single (Mrs David M.) Married'.

And what of the 'young master' these days? In my pre-teens childhood I can remember receiving letters and cards addressed to 'Master Nigel Rees'. Nowadays, first name and surname alone seem sufficient for the young master. 'Miss Suzanne Rees' is still current usage for a girl of any age, though it may wane. Formerly, the unrevealing 'Miss Rees' was used to describe the eldest daughter if there was more than one girl in a family, the younger daughter or daughters being identified by their first names as well as surname.

Now I know that not everyone will agree with me as I attempt to straighten out all these problems, major and minor, by my pragmatic, egalitarian approach. Such people are perfectly entitled to use whatever titles they feel comfortable with. By doing so, however, they run into even more problems. When they address a woman as 'Mrs Elizabeth Bristol', are they sure that she is divorced? Or do they think perhaps she is a married woman who has consciously chosen the 'married professional woman' way of referring to herself? When they address 'Mrs Peter Plymouth', are they sure she likes being addressed as the appendage of her husband rather than 'Sue Freelance' which is, in fact, the name she goes by professionally? When they address her using the title she herself has put on a letter to them '(Signed) E. Bristol (Mrs)', are they sure that she really knows what she is doing?

Mislaid in the mails

Malcolm Muggeridge wrote of Evelyn Waugh that he 'looked like a letter delivered to the wrong address' and there is something very woeful about correspondence that has not reached its intended destination. The Post Office asks you to: 'Just write your own address on the back of the envelope. Then, if for any reason we cannot deliver your letter, we can simply send it back to you – unopened and without delay.' Few people do this for domestic mails, though it is almost standard practice when writing to overseas addresses (see page 20).

A letter from Italy once reached the chemist Sir Humphry Davy (d. 1829) although it only bore the words, 'SIROMFREDEVI, LONDRA'. On another occasion, some friends of Mark Twain's wished to send him birthday greetings but, as he was on his travels, they did not know where to address the card. They put 'Mark Twain, God Knows Where' on the envelope and a few weeks later received Twain's acknowledgement: 'He did.' This sort of things strains the ingenuity and patience of the Post Office and should not be relied on.

In the beginning . . .

'Dear . . .' has been the commonest way of starting a letter since the seventeenth century and is, oddly, just as appropriate for addressing a total stranger as it is for an intimate. The addition of 'My' before the 'dear' certainly makes the salutation a little cosier – particularly between relatives, say – but usually has more to say about the relative warmth of the writer's personality than anything else.

But 'Dear *what*?' I advise a simple approach to titles: ignore most of them. Only use them where it would be outstandingly rude not to do so, or when the person addressed is perceived as being the kind who likes them. In other words, you should address people as they themselves would like to be addressed.

For the vast majority of people one is likely to have to deal with in correspondence, ignoring titles in these democratic days is a wonderfully refreshing thing to do and overcomes any number of niggling associated problems.

Similarly, if you start a letter in what used to be thought of as 'BBC' form, 'Dear Nigel Rees', it obviates having to worry whether it should be Miss, Mrs or Ms. This approach also lessens the likelihood of wrongly-sexing the recipient. There is something particularly unwinning about a mailshot addressed to a woman that begins 'Dear Sir', or addressed to a man that begins 'Dear Sir or Madam'. Indeed, 'Dear Sir or Madam' and 'Dear Sir/Madam' are curiously ungracious openings at the best of times, whatever the nature of the correspondence, and should be avoided at all costs.

Now I know that not everyone likes the 'Dear Tony Snodgrass' form. It is a bit clumsy, it is not ideal, but it helps considerably in overcoming certain technical matters.

One particular way of overcoming doubts about what degree of familiarity to adopt when addressing a correspondent is to rely simply on initials. 'Dear K.M.' and 'Dear J.G.' were the customary beginnings of letters between Joyce Grenfell and Katharine Moore (which will be referred to again later). To my mind this is the most delightful blend of the formal and informal. It is both one and the other, at the same time. I know it may sound a touch civil servantish or schoolmasterly (I always think of my teachers in terms of their initials, and, indeed, I can hardly recognize my old school pals if they do not use their initials), but it seems to work and can be recommended without hesitation.

It should be said that there are some etiquette gurus who deplore the omission of titles, honorifics and designations of any kind – it reduces everyone to the level of schoolchildren, so they say – but I do not find that this is so. What I do find is that addressing someone in a letter as

'Mr —— ——', instead of '—— ——, Esq.' is, in a way that I can't explain, not very complimentary.

But what if you are writing to someone whose name you may not know (like the bank manager) or if you are writing to an institution? Simple. If you begin, 'Dear Manager' or 'Dear Midland Bank'(even if you are not in the habit of addressing bricks and mortar) you can end with 'Yours sincerely' rather than the 'Yours faithfully' that should end a letter beginning 'Dear Sir'.

How would you address a letter to a group of mixed sex? 'Dear Sirs and Mesdames', 'Gentlepersons' and the Shakespearean 'gentles All' can probably be ruled out. 'Dear People' is, I believe, an occasional American locution, but sounds a bit grand – as if spoken from a platform or presidential balcony.

If you do not know what a person's initials stand for, then you can start with 'Dear X.Y. Zed' or 'Dear P.T. Brown'. Also, if you can't work out what sex a person is supposed to be from the name, you can hide your ignorance by putting 'Dear Min Scott' or 'Dear Branham Cox'.

There is also another way round the problem – don't put any salutation at all; just start in on the meat of your communication. This is easier to accomplish if you are writing on a postcard or small compliments slip-type sheet, but it is worth considering. The art of faxmanship would also appear to require this type of informality. If you take the view that the whole point of faxes is that they are not letters, then putting 'Dear Sir' and 'Yours faithfully' and pretending that they are is pointless.

Ah, Sweet Ms.tery of life

What about the 'Miss/Mrs/Ms' problem? 'Ms' (pronounced *miz*) is 'a title substituted for "Mrs" or "Miss" before a woman's name to avoid making a distinction between married and unmarried women', according to the *Collins Dictionary of the English Language* (1979). Thus it is a compromise (between 'Mrs' and 'Miss'), designed to solve a problem, and surely sounds every bit like the compromise it is. 'Ms' became popular with feminists in about 1970 at the start of the modern thrust by the Women's Movement. The New York Commission on Human Rights adopted it for use in correspondence at about that time. By 1972 a feminist magazine called *Ms* was being launched. The idea had been around for some time before it became – in the words of the *Oxford*

English Dictionary (Second Edition) – 'an increasingly common, but not universally accepted, use'.

This, from the early 1950s:

Use the abbreviation Ms for *all women* addressees. This modern style solves an age-old problem. – *The Simplified Letter*, National Office Management Association, Philadelphia, 4 January 1952

But it created a new problem. In August 1984 Geraldine Ferraro was the first woman to be selected as an American vice-presidential candidate. In what is known as 'private life', she was, in fact, Mrs John Zaccaro. In public she declined to be known as 'Miss Ferraro', feeling this was inapposite for a woman who was the mother of three children. She asked that she be called either 'Ms' or 'Mrs' Ferraro.

The *New York Times* in its traditional way, found this very hard to swallow. The paper liked to attach honorifics to names but did not permit the use of Ms in its columns and had to call her 'Mrs Ferraro' – despite pleadings from its own word expert, William Safire, who protested that 'Mrs Ferraro' was 'a person she is not. . . . It is unacceptable for journalists to dictate to a candidate that she call herself Miss or else use her married name.' In 1986 the newspaper gave way. But one can understand its reluctance to accept 'Ms' – not for opposing the motives behind its creation, but because it is not an elegant coinage. Many people seem quite happy to use it, nevertheless.

Couples

How do you address a couple? At a time when many people live together as couples and are not married, it is rather slack to address a card or invitation to them as 'Bob Bloke and Jane' or, for that matter, as 'Grizelda Mate and Dick' and as 'Hermione Mate and Liz'. You are probably doing this because you have never quite caught the partner's surname. So find out what it is. Putting only the name of the person you do know on the envelope and 'Bob and Jane' inside is artful but still sleight of hand.

Is it all right to use a person's first name when starting a letter, especially if you have not yet got round to doing so in conversation? It is almost a cliché of polite letter-writing to begin a letter with 'Dear Nigel (if I may)/(if I may make so bold/if I may be so familiar)'. There is nothing wrong with this, but be sensitive to the likely feelings of the person you are writing to. First-name familiarity will offend few people these days, but you can never be quite sure, especially when dealing with older people.

If typing either a personal or business letter, it is a nice touch to hand write the 'Dear . . .' (and the 'Yours . . .'), but don't do what a lot of people do, which is to type 'Dear' and then hand write the name. This has quite the reverse of the friendly effect intended and makes the letter look like a pro-forma one.

Writing to 'Lawrence of Arabia'/T.E. Lawrence during his self-effacing days in the RAF, Noël Coward began a letter: 'Dear 338171 (May I call you 338?)' – *Letters to T.E. Lawrence*, ed. D. Garnett (1938)

Facing the final curtain

Which brings us to the question of 'Yours etc . . .'. Do you end a letter by writing 'Yours faithfully' or 'Yours sincerely'? Frankly, I dislike 'Yours faithfully'. It speaks from a different age – of knights in armour and blood oaths and all that paraphernalia – and yet Correct Form dictates that if you begin a letter 'Dear Sir/Madam', you must end 'Yours faithfully'. By beginning 'Dear Person's Name', as suggested above, however, you avoid this necessity and can sign off 'Yours sincerely'.

Personally, I would seldom end with any of the variants like 'Yours truly', 'Yours very truly', 'Yours cordially' (Beachcomber recommended the response 'Dear Limejuice' to this one), 'Yours ever', 'Ever yours' (all right between very old acquaintances, but a bit wet with it), or 'Yours aye' (surely the province of Scots only?). 'Yours' on its own, while conveniently non-committal, is a pretty tepid way out. 'Yours affectionately' is probably only permissible between relations.

A servant of King George IV who wrote him a letter beginning 'My dearest sir' ended it 'invariably yours' (but joking with the sovereign is best avoided except by those who know exactly how it will be received). You can even avoid the matter entirely by signing off with 'Best wishes' or 'All good wishes' and eschewing a 'Yours' of any kind.

These days, almost anybody will attempt to get away with 'Love from . . .' or 'With Love'. This does not bear thinking about and, of course, should not – but will – be done.

In the Gowers revision of H.W. Fowler's *A Dictionary of Modern Usage* (1968), a more-or-less complete list of other moribund letter forms is given:

- I am, Sir . . .
- Believe me (to be) . . .
- I remain . . .
- I have the honour to be, with great truth and respect/with the highest consideration, Sir/Your Excellency/My Lord, your Excellency's/Your Lordship's obedient servant . . .
- I avail myself of this opportunity to renew to your Excellency the assurance of my highest consideration . . .
- Your obedient servant . . .
- Yours obediently . . .
- Yours respectfully . . .
- Yours to command . . .

Whichever form you choose, it is unlikely to go unnoticed. When Norma Major first went to Downing Street as the wife of the Prime Minister, John Major, she was quoted as saying this: 'As you go further up the ladder, people's attitudes change. I've noticed that people who used to sign themselves "love from" now use "yours sincerely" and that's a shame.'

Signatures

As for your signature, you will, naturally, put whatever you have evolved as your customary squiggle. Whether or not this is legible or intelligible in itself is neither here nor there, but it is obviously of importance that, if it is not, some additional explanation be given. In other words, print or type your name afterwards. It is only sensible that this second printed version should accord with the handwritten. You may well sign yourself 'Patricia Brett' and then put in brackets (Mrs P.E. Brett). This is correct, but it does not help if the hand-written signature is illegible (only you may be aware that the squiggle of ink actually denotes 'Patricia'.) To type or print the whole lot, repeating the name as signed, may seem rather officious, but it is well worth doing, especially if, say, you are sending a letter to a newspaper.

It may depend on what official signature you have evolved – for cheque-signing purposes, probably – but on the whole it is rather frosty to sign a letter using your initials rather than a forename. 'Yours sincerely, W.P. Thomas' is stiff; 'Yours sincerely, W.P. Thomas (Mrs)' reduces you to a cypher, a statistic, a mere address label.

Correct forms of address

The correct way in which you should write to people with titles or some other form of handle to their names, or who occupy a particular position in public life, can be difficult to establish. What follows, in democratically alphabetical order, is a list – though not an all-inclusive list – of such people, and guidance – no more than guidance – on what to do.

As with other forms of etiquette, modes of address are not set in cement. Usage develops, most notably towards a more informal style. Hence, in the list, most *formal* modes of address have been excluded as these belong to a bygone age. The chances are that most people will never even meet, let alone have reason to write to a duke, so it would seem pointless to draw attention to the very formal ways of addressing him.

Probably, the point to make is that though there are very definite things you should *not* do in this field, there is some choice in what you *may* do. The chief thing is not to be overawed by it. People don't really mind if you get things wrong and usually they will be very happy to tell you what they believe is right or what they expect (which may not be the same).

Another method is to check with *Debrett's People of Today* or with *Who's Who*, especially for those with complicated mixtures of title, rank and honour. It would be impossible to provide a guide which took account of every eventuality.

ADMIRAL (also for ADMIRAL OF THE FLEET,
VICE ADMIRAL, REAR ADMIRAL)
On envelope: 'Admiral of the Fleet/Vice Admiral/Rear Admiral, (Sir Horatio Fish)'
Starting letter: 'Dear Admiral' or 'Dear Admiral Fish' or Dear Sir Horatio', as appropriate

AIR CHIEF MARSHAL
On envelope: 'Air Chief Marshal (Sir David Flight)'
Starting letter: 'Dear (Sir David)'

AIR COMMODORE
On envelope: 'Air Commodore (W.A. Heron)'
Starting letter: 'Dear Air Commodore (Heron)'

AIR MARSHAL

On envelope: 'Air Marshal (F.O. Ward/Sir Frank Ward)'
Starting letter: 'Dear Air Marshal (Ward)/'(Sir Frank)'

AIR VICE MARSHAL

As for Air Marshal, except that the 'Vice' is always incorporated.

AMBASSADOR (British or foreign)

On envelope: As appropriate, 'His Excellency, HM Ambassador to ———' [only when in the accredited country] or 'His Excellency, The (British) Ambassador' or 'His Excellency, Sir (Richard Matt), KCMG' or 'His Excellency (Derek Diplo), CMG'
Starting letter: 'Dear (Sir Richard)' or 'Dear Mr (Diplo)' or (formally) 'Sir', or according to rank

ARCHBISHOP (Anglican)

On envelope: 'His Grace the Lord Archbishop of ———' or (less formally) 'The Most Rev. and Rt Hon. the Lord Archbishop of ———'
Starting letter: 'Your Grace', 'Dear Lord Archbishop', 'Dear Archbishop', as occasion demands

ARCHDEACON

On envelope: 'The Venerable The Archdeacon of ——— '
Starting letter: 'Dear Archdeacon/Mr Archdeacon' (a formal letter would begin 'Venerable Sir')

BARON (see also LIFE PEER)

On envelope: 'The Rt Hon. The Lord ———' (or socially) 'The Lord ———'
Starting letter: 'Dear Lord ———'

BARONESS (wife of Baron; see also LIFE PEERESS)

On envelope: 'The Lady ———'
Starting letter: 'Dear Lady ———'

BARONET

On envelope: 'Sir (Richard Heep), Bt.' (sometimes 'Bart.')
Starting letter: 'Dear Sir (Richard)'

BISHOP

On envelope: 'The Rt Rev. The Lord Bishop of ———'

N.B. The Bishop of London is 'The Rt Rev. and Rt Hon. The Lord Bishop of London'. Not all bishops are lord bishops. And there is another exception: The Bishop of Meath – the Premier Bishop of Ireland – is 'The Most Rev. . . .'
Starting letter: 'Dear Lord Bishop' or 'Dear Bishop'

BRIGADIER
On envelope: 'Brigadier (P.O. Popp)'
Starting letter: 'Dear Brigadier (Popp)'

CADET (Royal Navy)
On envelope: '(J.A. Tar) Esq. RN'
Starting letter: 'Dear Mr (Tar)'

CANON
On envelope: 'The Rev. Canon —— '
Starting letter: 'Dear Canon ——' (a very formal letter would begin 'Reverend Sir')

CAPTAIN (Army)
On envelope: 'Captain (V.R. Brave)' followed by name of regiment
Starting letter: 'Dear Captain (Brave)'

CAPTAIN (Royal Navy)
On envelope: 'Captain (J.A. Tar), RN'
Starting letter: 'Dear Captain (Tar)'

CHIEF RABBI
On envelope: 'The Chief Rabbi Dr —— ——'
Starting letter: 'Dear Chief Rabbi'

CLERGY (including MINOR CANONS, RURAL DEANS)
On envelope: 'The Rev. (O. Slope)' or 'The Reverend (O. Slope), if you think this looks better
Starting letter: 'Dear Mr (Slope)' (*not* 'Reverend (Slope)') or, where called for, 'Dear Father (Slope)'

COLONEL
On envelope: 'Colonel (O.T. Lunch)'
Starting letter: 'Dear Colonel (Lunch)'

COMMANDER

On envelope: 'Commander (J.A. Tar), RN'
Starting letter: 'Dear Commander (Tar)'
A Lieutenant Commander is addressed accordingly, with his rank abbreviated to 'Lt Cdr' on the envelope. A Royal Navy Lieutenant is addressed similarly.

COMMODORE

On envelope: 'Commodore (A.B. Parker)'
Starting letter: 'Dear Commodore (Parker)'

COUNTESS

On envelope: 'The Countess of ——'
Starting letter: 'Dear Countess of ——' or 'Dear Lady ——'

DAME

On envelope: 'Dame (Joan Davis) GBE' (or decoration as appropriate)
Starting letter: 'Dear Dame (Joan)'

DEAN (except RURAL DEAN, for which see CLERGY)

On envelope: 'The Very Rev. The Dean of ——'
Starting letter: 'Very Rev. Sir' or 'Dear Mr Dean' or 'Dear Dean'

DIVORCED WIFE OF PEER OR BARONET

She is known as, for example, 'Emma, Duchess of Tewkesbury'. If she remarries, she loses the title completely.

DUCHESS (see also ROYALS for Royal Duchesses)

On envelope: 'Her Grace, The Duchess of ——' or 'The Duchess of ——'
Starting letter: 'Dear Duchess of ——' or 'Dear Duchess'

DUKE (see also ROYALS for Royal Dukes)

On envelope: 'His Grace, The Duke of ——' or 'The Duke of ——'
Starting letter: 'Dear Duke of ——' or (familiarly) 'Dear Duke'

EARL

On envelope: 'The Rt Hon. Earl of ——' or 'The Earl of ——'
Starting letter: 'Dear Earl of ——' or 'Dear Lord ——'

ELDEST GRANDSON
OF DUKE OR MARQUESS
He takes his grandfather's third title, hence the grandson of a duke might be an earl. Oddly enough, on an envelope these people should be addressed without the 'the' – hence, 'Earl ————', which distinguishes them from actual holders of these ranks.

ELDEST SON OF
DUKE, MARQUESS OR EARL
He takes his father's secondary title: the son of a duke is a marquess, the son of a marquess is an earl, and the son of an earl is a viscount. The envelope rule holds as for the previous entry.

FIELD-MARSHAL
On envelope: 'Field-Marshal (Lord ——)'
Otherwise according to rank or title.

FLIGHT LIEUTENANT
On envelope: 'Flight Lieutenant (R.A. Eff)'
Starting letter: 'Dear Flight Lieutenant (Eff)'
For Air Force ranks below this, titles are not used.

GENERAL, LIEUTENANT-GENERAL, MAJOR
GENERAL
On envelope: 'General/Lt-Gen/Major General (Sir Marmaduke Gunn)'
Starting letter: 'Dear General (Gunn)' or 'Dear (Sir Marmaduke)'

GROUP CAPTAIN
On envelope: 'Group Captain (R.A. Eff)'
Starting letter: 'Dear Group Captain (Eff)'

HON. (HONOURABLE)
On envelope: 'The Hon. Mr/Mrs/Miss —— ——'
Starting letter: 'Dear Mr/Mrs/Miss ——'
Note that the word 'Hon.' is never written out in full.

JUDGE (Circuit)
On envelope: 'His/Her Honour Judge ——' (or, with additional title, e.g. 'His Honour Sir —— ——')
Starting letter: 'Dear Judge ——' or 'Dear Sir/Madam'

JUDGE (High Court)
On envelope: 'The Hon. Mr/Mrs Justice (Probity)' or (privately) 'Sir (Eric Probity)' or 'Dame (Elizabeth Probity)', as appropriate
Starting letter: 'Dear Sir/Madam'

JUSTICES OF THE PEACE
Only on the bench would a Justice be addressed as 'Your Worship'. The initials 'JP' would only be put after the name on official business.

KNIGHT
As for Baronet, except that if he is a member of an order, this should be put on an envelope, e.g. 'Sir Desmond Gribble KBE, CMG'. The wife of a knight is addressed as for a baronet's wife.

LIEUTENANT, SECOND LIEUTENANT (Army)
On envelope: '(N.O. Action) Esq.' (rank used only on official envelopes)
Starting letter: 'Dear Mr (Action)'

LIEUTENANT (Royal Navy) (see COMMANDER)

LIEUTENANT COLONEL
On envelope: 'Lieut.-Colonel (De'Ath)' followed by any decorations, followed by the name of the regiment
Starting letter: 'Dear Colonel (De'Ath)'

LIEUTENANT COMMANDER (see
COMMANDER)

LIEUTENANT-GENERAL (see GENERAL)

LIFE PEER (i.e. non-hereditary)
On envelope: 'The Rt Hon. the Lord ——' (or socially) 'The Lord ——'
Starting letter: 'Dear Lord ——'
N.B. The full title 'Lord Jones of Smethwick' is never used. The wife of a male life peer is 'The Lady ——' and should be addressed similarly, not as a life peeress.

LIFE PEERESS (i.e. non-hereditary BARONESS)
On envelope: 'The Rt Hon. the Baroness ——' (or socially) 'The Baroness ——' or even 'Baroness ——'
Starting letter: 'Dear Lady ——'

N.B. There is a tendency in the media to refer to 'Baroness ——', with the aim of distinguishing her as a political figure in her own right from the appendage of her husband the 'Lady' form might suggest.

LORD MAYOR

On envelope: 'The Right Worshipful the Lord Mayor of ——' – except in special cases (e.g. London, York and Belfast) where it is 'The Rt Hon. the Lord Mayor of ——'
Starting letter: 'My Lord' or 'Dear Lord Mayor'
Writing to a Lord Mayor's wife or to a Lady Mayoress, put 'The Lady Mayoress', or use private rank.)
Compare MAYOR – and do not confuse with.

MAJOR

On envelope: 'Major (T.R. Rex)' followed by name of regiment
Starting letter: 'Dear Major (Rex)'

MAJOR GENERAL (See GENERAL)

MARCHIONESS

On envelope: 'The Marchioness of ——'
Starting letter: 'Dear Marchioness of ——' or 'Dear Lady ——'

MARQUESS

On envelope: 'The Marquess of ——'
Starting letter: 'Dear Marquess of —— or 'Dear Lord ——'

MARSHAL OF THE ROYAL AIR FORCE

On envelope: 'Marshal of the Royal Air Force (Lord Wing)'
Otherwise according to rank and title.

MAYOR

On envelope: 'The Right Worshipful the Mayor of ——' (if of a city) or 'The Worshipful the Mayor of ——' (if of a borough, etc.)
Starting letter: 'Dear Mr Mayor' or 'Dear Mr (Chain)' or 'Dear Mrs (Chain)'

MIDSHIPMAN

On envelope: 'Midshipman (J.A. Tar) RN' or '(J.A. Tar) Esq. RN'
Starting letter: 'Dear Mr (Tar)'

MINOR CANON (see CLERGY)

PEER, PEERESS (See LIFE PEER, LIFE PEERESS)

POPE

On envelope: 'His Holiness the Pope (Nigel Thomas II).'
Starting letter: 'Your Holiness' or 'Most Holy Father'

PREBENDARY

Follows the form for CANON.

PRESIDENT (of the United States)

On envelope: 'The President of the United States'
Starting letter: 'Dear Mr President' or 'Sir' / 'Madam' ('Dear
Madam President', when that day comes.

It has become customary in recent years for ex-Presidents to be referred to in public affairs and in their presence as 'President ——', though properly there is only one 'President of the United States' at any one time. Dwight D. Eisenhower reverted to 'General' when he left office.

PRIME MINISTER

On envelope: 'The Rt Hon. —— ——, PC, MP'
Starting letter: 'Dear Prime Minister' or 'Dear Mr/Mrs
——'

Other members of the government follow this pattern, whether 'Chancellor' (of the Exchequer), 'Secretary of State' or 'Minister'. Former Prime Ministers do not retain the title.

PROFESSOR

On envelope: 'Prof.' or 'Professor —— ——'
Starting letter: 'Dear Professor'

PROVOST

Follows the form for DEAN.

QUEEN, THE

On envelope: 'The Private Secretary to Her Majesty The
Queen' – she should rarely be written to direct.
Starting letter: Hence 'Dear Sir' (otherwise 'Your Majesty')
(see also ROYALS)

REAR ADMIRAL (see ADMIRAL)

ROYALS

Generally speaking, the rule to remember is that when writing to or about members of the Royal Family, personal pronouns should not be used. So you write 'Your Majesty' or 'Her Majesty' or 'The Queen' rather than 'you' or 'her'; 'Your Royal Highness' or 'Her Royal Highness' rather than 'you' or 'her'. However, the changes may be rung to lessen any tendency to sound pompous and preposterous. Also, relationships are best not rubbed in. The Queen's grandfather, for example, would be referred to as 'King George V' rather than 'your grandfather'.

People who are a little more familiar with royalty might feel like beginning a letter 'Ma'am', 'Madam' or 'Sir', if they did not want to go the whole hog of 'Your Majesty' or 'Your Royal Highness'. However, signing off is a difficult matter. 'I have the honour to be, Your Majesty's/Your Royal Highness's most humble and obedient servant' would stick in the pen of the most loyal subject these days. Starting with 'Madam' and ending 'Yours faithfully' will not cause the Queen to send you to the Tower these days; similarly 'Dear Duchess' and 'Yours sincerely' is unlikely to alienate a Duchess of York.

Addressing the envelope: the form is quite straightforward, but note (from this incomplete list) where capital letters and commas are put. Ideally, the 'His/Her Royal Highness' should be written in full:

Her Majesty, Queen Elizabeth, The Queen Mother
HRH The Duke of Edinburgh *or* HRH Prince Philip, The Duke of Edinburgh
(in both the above cases, as with The Queen, letters should properly be addressed to 'The Private Secretary to . . .')
HRH The Prince of Wales HRH The Princess of Wales
HRH Prince William of Wales
HRH Prince Henry (Harry) of Wales
HRH The Princess Royal
HRH Princess Alexandra, the Hon. Lady Ogilvy
HRH The Duke of York
HRH Princess Beatrice of York
HRH Princess Eugenie of York

HRH The Prince Edward

HRH Prince Michael of Kent

HRH The Princess Margaret, Countess of Snowdon

Of the princes, only The Prince of Wales and The Prince Edward have 'The' after HRH. This is because they are sons of the sovereign. Prince Michael of Kent, for this reason, is not 'The Prince Michael' because he is not a son of the sovereign. Note that 'HRH The Prince Philip' is less often used than 'HRH The Duke of Edinburgh', but the 'The' is in place as he is married to the sovereign.

Of the princesses, note that The Princess Royal has 'The' but HRH Princess Alexandra does not, for the same reason.

Letters to the foregoing, where they are addressed direct, should begin, 'Your Royal Highness'.

RURAL DEAN (see CLERGY)

SECOND LIEUTENANT (Army) (see LIEUTENANT)

SQUADRON LEADER
On envelope: 'Squadron Leader (R.A. Eff)'
Starting letter: 'Dear Squadron Leader (Eff)'

SUB-LIEUTENANT (Royal Navy)
On envelope: 'Sub-Lieutenant (J.A. Tar) RN'
Starting letter: 'Dear Mr (Tar)'

UNMARRIED DAUGHTER OF DUKE, MARQUESS OR EARL
She is known as 'Lady (Laura Stanley)' and is addressed accordingly.

VICE ADMIRAL (see ADMIRAL)

VISCOUNT
On envelope: 'The Rt Hon. the Viscount ——' or 'The Viscount ——'
Starting letter: 'Dear Viscount ——' or 'Dear Lord ——'

VISCOUNTESS
On envelope: 'The Viscountess ——'
Starting letter: 'Dear Viscountess ——' or 'Dear Lady ——'

WIDOW OF PEER OR BARONET

She is addressed as when her husband was alive, except where the present peer is married, in which case her first name is put first, as in '(Alice), Duchess of (Slimbridge)'. Should there be two widowed ladies with the same title, the senior is called 'The Dowager Duchess of (Slimbridge)', or whatever.

WING COMMANDER

On envelope: 'Wing Commander (R.A. Eff)'
Starting letter: 'Dear Wing Commander (Eff)'

YOUNGER SON OF DUKE OR MARQUESS

He is known as 'Lord —— ——' (e.g. Lord David Tite) and is addressed as 'Lord (David)' and written to familiarly as 'Lord (David)', the envelope being addressed to 'Lord (David Tite)'. His wife is addressed, accordingly, as 'Lady (David Tite)'.

YOUNGER SON OF EARL, SON OF VISCOUNT OR BARON

On envelope: 'Hon. Stephen Borrow' (the 'the' is properly omitted)
Starting letter: 'Dear Mr Borrow'
Accordingly his wife is 'Hon. Mrs (Stephen) Borrow'.

Letters after the name

Except in the most formal of communications, it is probably best to forgo letters after a person's name, especially as deciding on the precise order is a very complicated business. Broadly speaking, the order is: decorations (CBE, etc.); appointments (PC, for Privy Counsellor, etc.); legal appointments (QC, JP, etc.); university degrees (MA, etc.); religious orders (SJ, for Society of Jesus); medical qualifications (FRCS, Fellow of the Royal College of Surgeons); membership of learned societies (RA, for Royal Academy); member of parliament (MP); membership of armed forces (RN, etc.).

Getting the title right is the most important thing (Lord, Sir, Rt Hon., Dr, or whatever) and that will probably suffice in most cases. However, if a person does not have a title (other than Esq., Mr, Mrs, Ms), you should consider whether your remembering their OBE would make them happy. A label like MP should always be used. University degrees should not normally be put, though non-medical doctorates may be brandished in an academic context. Proud parents will probably ignore this advice and never fail to mention a doctorate or other degree (at least until the novelty wears off).

The intricacies of such matters may be more fully explored in *Debrett's Peerage and Baronetage*. As already mentioned, another publication, *Debrett's People of Today*, solves many queries on this score as each individual listed is given a personal 'style' which you can assume is correct, otherwise he or she would not have approved it.

5

DROPPING A LINE

This chapter is concerned with social and personal mail – the sort that you initiate yourself rather than simply reply to. I am always reminded of just what we have lost through the use of the telephone for so much of our day-to-day communication when I read the letters, or notes, that Sir Richard Steele, the eighteenth-century essayist, used to dash off to his wife, *whatever* he was up to:

> I am come to a tavern alone to eat a steak, after which I shall return to the office. – 28 October 1707 (when they had been married for less than two months. Of course, in those good old days, such letters were taken by messenger and had an instant quality about them)

> I was going home two hours ago, but was met by Mr Griffith, who has kept me ever since. I will come within a pint of wine. – eleven at night, 5 January 1708

> A little in drink, but at all times yr faithful husband. – 27 September 1708

These are, if you like, the equivalent of the modern phone call, but not the *same*. The fact that the thought or message has been written down and conveyed by a third party somehow invests the process with an extra quality. It is imbued with the romance, in fact, of letter sending. We would all be the better off if we could recapture some of that sensation.

Pop it in the post

How should social and personal correspondence differ from business mail? As much as possible, without quite losing *all* formality. Writing a letter *is* a rather formal thing to do, whatever the occasion for it and even if the subject is an intimate one. The act of writing on a piece of paper and sending it off on a small voyage to another person is not the same as speaking directly to that person and it is wrong to pretend otherwise. It is, if you like, a rather artificial process but that should not stop you from trying to recreate yourself in the words that you write. So, be yourself when you write a personal letter. You are not making a speech to the golf club annual dinner.

Put the date on your letter. However long a letter may last, it is still the product of a moment in time and it is well worth pinpointing that moment. As for greater informality in notepaper design and quality, think twice before indulging in anything too whacky. Personalized pink stuff with cherubs may be all very well for love letters but you are going to need something else upon which to write to the bank manager. Similarly, a letterhead, and especially one printed with your name, may not set the required tone of intimacy for a personal note. For this reason, it is as well to keep some blank sheets of paper to hand.

Postcards only, please

Postcards, whether blank or printed with your name and address on (also called 'correspondence cards'), are an ideal way of dealing with small matters – not least for briefly acknowledging something or simply saying thank you, without having to write a full-blown letter. As these do not require a 'Dear ——' at the start of the message, nor a 'Yours ——' at the end, they are also a good way of sidestepping the problem of just how to address your correspondent.

On the other hand, postcards are a rather public form of communication – anyone can read them – but there is nothing to stop you from putting them in envelopes. That way you also gain more writing space on the card because you don't have to put the address of the person you are writing to.

If you are sending a picture postcard with a thank-you message, it is not necessary to put your address on it, though if the postcard is of a foreign place or not of a place at all, it might be as well to write the name of your home town to make it clear where you are writing from.

If a printed postcard already bears your name, this is sufficient indication and you can safely use just your initial or initials to sign off with.

It might be thought that a postcard is too casual for some types of thank-you message – those requiring the full treatment. Putting the postcard within an envelope may lessen the accusation of casualness.

Theatricals are great senders of little messages – of good luck on first nights, of thanks for almost anything, of congratulations – and it is one of their more agreeable traits. The use of a postcard or correspondence card makes this sending ever so much easier to do than writing a formal letter. Even in business or professional life, the sending of little notes of encouragement, appreciation or congratulation can work wonders. In broadcasting I can recall a senior executive who almost always sent you a little handwritten note after a programme – to such an extent that it came to seem like an inevitable ritual. But I certainly noticed when someone else took over his job and never, ever bothered to do such a thing.

Wish you were here

Holiday postcards are a curious ritual and it is hard for even the most inspired sender not to fall into the 'Wish you were here/hope you are keeping well/the x shows our hotel bedroom' mode. The main thing, though, is that you have remembered to send a card and nobody is very interested to know whether you are enjoying yourself in the sun, or not. I detect a trend these days not to impart any information at all but simply to write 'Best wishes from . . .' in as large letters as it takes to fill up the space.

Terribly well-organized people who set off on holiday intending to buy postcards and then use pre-printed stickers with their friends' addresses on them run the risk of turning what should be a kind thought into an industrial process.

Should you be nervous of dealing with foreign post offices and trusting your cards to the international mails, and should you rather not have your postcards arrive home three weeks after you do, it might be an idea to post them at home, as soon as you arrive there (with some such line as 'this is the PC I would have sent you if . . .'). But this should not become your usual mode of operation.

Post early for Christmas

The growing adoption of the American practice of including with your Christmas card a newsletter about the family's doings over the previous twelve months should be treated cautiously. Such newsletters are usually banal and written in a particularly irritating style, with rather too many medical details ('I survived triple-bypass surgery in April') and too many comments in brackets ('And guess who got to do that job!!') Best avoided, I say, or at least only sent out to the known forbearing. A scribbled line or two at the bottom of the card should suffice, but the tradition of the Christmas letter, bringing friends up to date on the past year dies hard.

Congratulations

Congratulations cost nothing and should be as much of a pleasure to give as to receive. Don't hold back.

SPECIMEN LETTER 5: CONGRATULATIONS ON ACHIEVEMENT

87, College Road
Bury St Edmunds
Suffolk
BS1 3XX

Tel. 0X45-5678901

12 June 199–

Dear Philip,

We were delighted to read of your CBE in the *Telegraph* this morning. Could anything have been more deserved? We are thrilled for you.

With much love from

Jennie and Paul

The birth of a baby is also cause for unequivocal rejoicing. Never mind if they (the happy couple) have too many children already, are on the point of splitting up, or are only likely to have given birth to a monster. Congratulation is the order of the day. Although, traditionally, there has been a tendency to address such letters to the mother only, I feel that such productions are joint efforts, and so:

SPECIMEN LETTER 6: CONGRATULATIONS ON BIRTH OF BABY

The Arbour
247, The Speedway
Chesterfield
Derbyshire
SH5 DR4

Telephone 0X3-3861034

28 December 199–

Dear Judy and Simon,

Congratulations! Sarah and I were so thrilled to hear about the latest addition to the Macdonald clan. We look forward to seeing him home very soon. Meanwhile, we hope that mother and baby are doing well . . .

With much love

Don and Georgina

This does not anticipate an invitation to the christening, a request to be a godparent, or anything else. It is straightforward, good-natured congratulation.

Letters to children

There is a specific art involved when writing to children. Some people resort to CAPITAL LETTERS IN THE BELIEF THAT THESE ARE EASIER TO READ, while others, more sensibly, think that early experience in deciphering grown-up handwriting is invaluable. A half-way house is to write in lower case but without joining the letters up. There is, nevertheless, a virtue in directness of expression when dealing with children. Irony is lost on them (as it is on so many adults), so say what you have to say, and then shut up . . .

SPECIMEN LETTER 7: TO A CHILD, ACCOMPANYING A PRESENT

> The Hydro
> 25, College Road East
> Brantley
> Cumbria
> CA6 2BX

18 December 199–

Dear Rusty,

I remember your saying when last we met that what you wanted more than anything else in the world was Sonic the Hedgehog, so here it is. I hope you haven't got one already!

Love from

Stephen

This said, I have to confess to a certain element of calculation if I want to receive a thank-you letter, or, at the very least, some acknowledgement that a present has been received. I have found that if my young friends have to consult their parents to obtain my address, or to post a thank-you letter to me, then that is the end of the matter: nothing ever comes. So I have taken to inserting with my presents a short handwritten note on my own notepaper (with my address on it, in other words) plus a crisp suggestion that they tell me what they are up to, their ambitions for the future, and so on. This hasn't failed to work – yet.

SPECIMEN LETTER 8: TO A CHILD, ABOUT NOTHING AT ALL

> 289, Main Stem Road
> Worcester
> Hereford and Worcester
> WO9 X35

Telephone: 03X3-456918

2 May 199–

My dear . . .

Have you ever wondered why Mummy and Daddy tell you not to climb on the cooker or walk on the window-ledges?

There's a simple reason which they may not have told you.

Outside your house, just across the stream, there's a sheep called 'BAA', isn't there? Well, I don't know if you've ever noticed but 'BAA' has great big ears. They are rather difficult to see, I agree. There's so much wool in the way.

But every time you jump off the window-ledge or knock down a pan from the shelf, *'BAA' can hear you!* And because she can hear you with those big ears of hers, she can't get to sleep.

And when 'BAA' can't get to sleep she can't produce any wool. And that means there aren't enough woolly clothes to keep you warm in the winter.

So next time Mummy or Daddy stops you from jumping or knocking things over or shouting 'Mince!' at the top of your voice, then remember it's all because of 'BAA'!

And although I live a long way away, I have big ears too – and you wouldn't want to frighten *me*, now would you?

Be good.

Much love from . . .

This was a letter I wrote to some extremely small young friends so long ago that I can't really remember why I did it. There appears to be some didactic purpose in the bits about not climbing on the cooker or jumping off window-ledges, but it is hard to tell. Despite what I say above, it was written in capital letters. It was also illustrated by drawings which I, being no Beatrix Potter, will not reproduce here. Children who do receive illustrated letters from people with artistic talent are blessed indeed.

When you write to children who are not yet able to read, you find yourself also sending little messages to the parents who you know will have to do the reading for them. A slight example: in the third volume of Harold Nicolson's *Diaries and Letters 1945-1962* (published in 1968), there is reproduced a delightful letter to his granddaughter, Juliet, aged seven weeks, just after her christening. It begins, 'Now that you have been admitted into the Church and had a paragraph all to yourself in the *Daily Telegraph*, you should be able, if not to read, then to take in, private letters.' But really it is addressed to Juliet's parents: 'And will you tell your other parent that I really believe that you will have large eyes as lovely as she has and a character as sweet as hers . . .'

Such letters can easily become mawkish and sentimental but they most certainly *should* be attempted. Inspired by that Nicolson letter, I recall writing to my nephew rather than to his father, when that father (my brother) asked me to be a godparent:

London NW1
18th August 1970

My dear James,

You can barely see, let alone read – but if I am to be your Godfather, you must prepare yourself from an early age to receive letters of worldly wisdom and advice from one who has such a lot of that to share with you. You and I have, of course, something which neither your father nor your mother knows the slightest thing about: the perils and delights of being a younger brother. However, you will be spared having to wear your sister's cast-off clothing. At least, I hope you will. If not, that is something I will have to speak to you about a little later on.

I am sending you, along with this letter, some of that vital substance without which you will not get very far in the world and I hope your parents will be wise enough to let you spend it at the earliest opportunity on whatever mad enthusiasm strikes you as being terribly important at the time. I had thought of expressing it in guineas, but they – alas – will be history by the time you are able to read this letter for yourself, so I shall have to make up the difference to you some other time – whilst, of course, maintaining towards your big sister that fairness and equality inculcated in me by your paternal grandparents.

Your christening is to be in October, I understand, so perhaps you would be so good as to tell your mother and father that I shall be pleased to be at the 'stand-up luncheon' beforehand. I hope I will still be in a position to attend your stand-up Christening afterwards. I additionally hope that you will be on your best behaviour then and always, while not neglecting to keep your parents firmly in their place.

With love from your affectionate uncle – and, shortly to be, god-father,

Nigel

This seems to have stood up quite well, though it is possibly a little too much aimed at entertaining the parents. Still, they kept the letter and my nephew is now just about capable of reading it for himself.

Begging letters

I will not tell you how to write these, as they shouldn't be sent (see, however, 'Charitable appeals', Chapter 9). But how to respond, if at all?

Since becoming an author, I have discovered that we, as a breed, are a particular target for begging-letter writers. And I thought everyone knew we were badly off? The most barefaced of these in recent years have been letters, chiefly from Africa and the Indian sub-continent, fishing for free copies of our works. Should you yourself wish to try this on, you may care to model your missive on this, which is a composite (mostly from Nigeria and India), complete with original spelling and grammar, but I would rather you didn't:

THE BEGAWANGA MARKETTING CORP.

18 August 199–.

Dear Nigel Rees,

We have the pleasure to know of your reputable company in publishing business. We are a manufacturing and long established marketting company.

We are prepared at all times to lend our experience assistance by way a normal business relationship. In other words we stand a better chance and in position of giving you a developed and viable market strong hold possibly in whole continent.

We therefore, request that you forward to us your brochures, quatation, samples and proforma invoice coupled with your terms of business. Be assured of our high cooperation result.

We anticipate your maximum co-operation and earliest reply with regards,

Yours sincerely . . .

And here is another, which may be from India or Nigeria also:

12 April 199–

Dear Mr Rees,

This letter has been overdue, and the compliments too! I very much appreciated your books . . . There was much to learn and treasure from both.

I teach English Language and Literature in a college of my region. I am interested in studying and reviewing your recent book. . . . Please do send me a signed copy. It'll be such a help to my students.

Thank you!

Do have a wonderful summer!

Warmest wishes,

Very sincerely yours . . .

I think this is what is known as 'neck'.

Penpals

As singles bars are to courtship, so penpals are to correspondence – they are an engineered way of achieving what you want to achieve. Presumably, in the latter case, what you want is friendship at a safe distance, to give and to receive information, and to get lots of envelopes with exotic foreign stamps on them. Pen friendships are often encouraged as a way of helping one, if not both, of the parties to overcome loneliness. They might involve a person in the services stationed in some remote and boring outpost, or one side of the correspondence might be in prison.

Whatever the case, they *can* be rewarding experiences. Joyce Grenfell, the actress, conducted a correspondence over twenty-two years with Katharine Moore, a woman she never actually met. Said Moore (older than Grenfell and a writer in her own right), 'We agreed long ago not to meet; we liked it better that way.' Their letters were eventually published as *An Invisible Friendship* (1982). Sir Dirk Bogarde, the actor, similarly, carried on a long correspondence with someone who likewise had originally written him a fan letter. Presumably what both these public personalities gained from the correspondence was a way of sharing their experiences with an uninvolved audience – but an audience that was more alive and responsive than the kind of posterity that reads a personal diary, for example.

The publisher Rupert Hart-Davis conducted a delightful correspondence with one of his former teachers, George Lyttelton, and it has also been published. At the time, Lyttelton was retired and Hart-Davis was in the thick of business life. The subject matter was mainly literary, but the overall feeling was one of an agreeable conversation. It helped Lyttelton keep in touch with the world and perhaps gave Hart-Davis a link with a calmer, more reflective life than he was leading at the time.

There is no doubt that a correspondence which is not about business or which is not hoping to foster a 'relationship' of whatever kind can be a very agreeable thing. I once fell into a correspondence with a much older man who had written to me out of the blue. His working life had a number of parallels with mine. We did eventually meet – indeed, we collaborated on a book together, by post – and I was deeply saddened by his death. I expect he enjoyed writing to someone who was still in the thick of life. I enjoyed writing to someone who was well out of it (but who had survived).

Of course, sometimes penpals do become rather more than that.

People claim to have fallen in love with each other through letters and progressed to matrimony, but that is expecting rather a lot.

At the most basic level, penfriendships are often encouraged between people of school age, particularly as a way of learning to write in a foreign language. This can be hard work for both sides.

There is no easy way to launch one of these rarely fruitful correspondences. I have experienced about three in my lifetime and wouldn't have missed them for the world. They are a life-line outside a conventional relationship and can be very reassuring and agreeable. If it is someone famous you would like to correspond with – and the chances of it taking off are minimal – then just try writing, at no great length, perhaps with some query, to see what the response will be. Good luck. You never know.

'Friendship is the great chain of human society, and intercourse of letters is one of the chiefest links of that chain.' – James Howell (1594?-1666), *Familiar Letters*

'Beasts may convey, and tuneful birds may sing,
Their mutual feelings, in the opening Spring;
But man alone has skill and power to send
The heart's warm dictates to the distant friend.' – George Crabbe, *The Library* (1781)

Letters of introduction

The letter of introduction is a time-honoured way of giving help to someone you know who may be about to travel abroad and needs putting in touch with friendly faces, or who is simply moving into a different environment and needs help. The letter does not need to be shown to the person whom it is designed to help but if it is of a general nature (like a reference) and will be carried by the person, then it should obviously not contain anything that the person would be offended by, should that person happen to see it. Envelopes containing letters of the last type should not be sealed.

SPECIMEN LETTER 9: INTRODUCING SOMEONE (i)

(This is a letter I actually received a year or two ago.)

Dear Nigel,

Remember me? You slept in my husband's dressing room when you visited Denver some years ago!

I have been promising myself I would look you up when in London but I have never been there for long enough. However, our daughter Holly is descending on London for some months (she was about seven when you last met her). She is a joy and has just completed her final year of an Honors Arts course majoring in History. She is claiming her reward – a year of travel.

I felt that you would be an ideal person for her to meet at this stage of her life so I have suggested she ring you in London. I would very much appreciate it, if you could give her a little of your time.

As for Harold and me . . . The last child moved out of the house a month ago, so we are intent on recapturing our lost youth (together) – perhaps we may even visit you!

Warmest regards,

Rather to my surprise, I found that appeal quite irresistible. The flattery is nicely pitched ('an ideal person for her to meet at this stage of her life' – very winning) and the reminder that I, in my youth, had been the recipient of their hospitality, was delicately inserted. Holly came to see us, she *was* a joy, and her parents followed soon after.

SPECIMEN LETTER 10: INTRODUCING SOMEONE (ii) – PROFESSIONAL

GLOBAL BUSINESS TRANSACTIONS
The Tower
The Headrow
Leeds
LS1 2XX

Tel. 0X34-789045

Barry Charman
The Business Corporation
243, Kingsway Strand
LONDON
WCX 1ED   2 March 199–

Dear Barry,

We have on our staff a young man called ―― ―― who began with us as a trainee and has risen successfully through the ranks. He now sees his future in ―― rather than in ――, with a bent and talent in that direction.

Although he has performed well for us in this new field, there probably isn't enough scope for him, at his age, to develop his skills further with us. But if any of your people are in the market for an enthusiastic and intelligent worker, I would be grateful if they could spare the time to see him.

All the best,

Geoffrey

(For business and professional references, see Chapter 7, page 110.)

SPECIMEN LETTER 11: INTRODUCING SOMEONE (iii)

[To whom it may concern]

This is to introduce Christine France. For the past five years or more, Christine has been known to us as a reliable and helpful family friend. She is now leaving us to work her way round the world.

May I ask you to give her as much assistance as you are able in whatever way she needs at any particular time? Should you wish to have confirmation of the veracity of this letter, then please do not hesitate to contact me by letter, phone or fax.

With my thanks for your anticipated help to Christine – which I am sure you will not regret.

Yours sincerely,

I suggest omitting the 'to whom it may concern' as that makes it sound far too official and legalistic. If you felt like putting 'Dear Friend', so be it. The main thing is that any such letter should be on printed notepaper, giving your address and phone number. If your name is printed on the paper, together with some indication of your domestic or professional status, so much the more valuable.

Alas, I have received similarly winning letters of introduction to people who were not a joy to have inflicted on me and, indeed, were something of an imposition. If I had suspected this, I might just have had the nerve to wriggle free by telling some whopper about being out of the country for months, in the midst of a severe domestic crisis, or some other such fib. Whatever your response, however, a letter of introduction *does* need to be acknowledged (except for the last type, obviously).

∾ 6 ∾

A REPLY IS IN THE POST

This chapter, like the previous one, is concerned with social and personal mail. Here, however, the focus is on letters which you are not initiating but merely replying to.

Are replies really necessary?

This sounds like one of those eternal debating topics like 'Is sex really necessary?' and is similarly hard to answer. Broadly speaking, the answer must be Yes, but all sorts of factors come in to the view that you will take – whether the letter clearly requires an answer, whether the sender expects one, whether you have the time and energy to supply one. Only if you really enjoy the business of correspondence will you fall to sending a reply by return and without thinking whether one is really necessary.

Lord Chesterfield wrote one of his famous (and faintly questionable) letters of advice (to his godson) on this very subject in 1768:

> My Dear Boy,
>
> I send you enclosed a letter from your friend young Mr Chenevix, which you should answer in about a month. Politeness is as much concerned in answering letters within a reasonable time, as it is in returning a bow, immediately. . . . Letters of business must be answered immediately, and are the easiest either to write or to answer, for the subject is ready and only requires great clearness and perspicuity in the treating. . . . The letters that are the hardest to write, are those that are upon no subject at all, which are like *Small Talk* in conversation. They admit of wit if you have any . . . but they should seem easy and natural, and not smell of the lamp.

'One complimentary letter asks another.' – English proverb (for example, in Thomas Nashe's *Have With You to Saffron Walden*, 1596: 'One complimentary letter asketh another; and Gabriell first writing to him, and seeming to admire him and his works, he could doo no lesse . . . but returne him an answere in the like nature.')

'I always feel "a letter should be answered".' – *The Diaries of Kenneth Williams*, entry for 4 January 1981 (1993)

The answer to the question 'Are replies really necessary?' is easier if a definite, specific question is put to you in the incoming missive, as in an invitation.

Replying to invitations

If you receive an utterly formal invitation, you are obliged to write, by hand, an utterly formal acceptance or refusal. However awkward it may seem, this must be in the third person:

> Mr John Alexander thanks Mrs Sebastian Frost for her kind invitation to an At Home on Friday April 2nd and has much pleasure in accepting.

Or:

> Mr John Alexander thanks Mrs Sebastian Frost for her kind invitation to an At Home on Friday April 2nd but very much regrets that he will be unable to attend.

Note that these replies do not have to replay *every* detail on the invitation. Nor does the answerer, in giving regrets for non-attendance, have to give any reason for his inability to attend. The letter is not signed, nor does it need to be dated.

However, as the formality of the original invitation declines, so may that of the response. If a telephone number is given for reply, you do not even have to write at all, though you may prefer to. If the invitation has only your first name written top left, then this is a signal that you do not have to reply in the third person. Indeed, you can now write a short note and loosen up considerably:

Dear Mrs Frost,

Thank you very much for your invitation for Friday 2nd. I am very much looking forward to being with you.

Yours sincerely . . .

Or:

Dear Mrs Frost,

Thank you very much for your invitation for Friday 2nd. Alas, I shall be away on holiday that week, not returning till the following day, and will be unable to come.

Many regrets,

Yours sincerely . . .

On the other hand, here is a very *informal* and quirky but complimentary acceptance of an invitation, sent by the historian Thomas Carlyle (1795-1881), just to show how this kind of thing can be carried off creatively and unstarchily. It was handwritten:

Dear Mrs Stanley,

Unless this poisonous easterly weather, and the paltriest set of nerves in the world, prove too hard for me, I will certainly come, – afraid only of being *too* happy!

Yours ever truly,

T. Carlyle

The chief thing to remember is that a speedy reply to an invitation is obligatory whether accepting or declining. If the function is a small dinner party for eight or a dance for four hundred, the host or hostess needs to know the numbers in good time for catering purposes. In addition, to delay replying might seem as if you were waiting for something better to turn up.

If you are genuinely unsure whether you will be free – and depending on the importance of the occasion – you should consider letting the inviter know what your position is. You *could* give a provisional acceptance and then absolutely not fail to confirm a little later whether you are actually going to attend or not. Whether it would be all right to decline and then seek a re-invitation, according to circumstances, I doubt.

For large drinks parties, where my actual presence or absence would hardly be noticed, I personally have sometimes found myself using the formula, '. . . am looking forward very much to being able to attend . . .' This implies some doubt as to whether I actually will or not. I suspect this is not very good form.

If a hostess does not receive a reply to a written invitation, she is entitled to assume that the person is not coming and to make other arrangements. The chances of the reply having been lost in the post are small. Should the invitee ring up at the last moment, the hostess is entitled to tell a white lie and say the event has been cancelled and offer a barbed, 'But thank you for letting me know, anyhow.'

Thinking of invitations in the broad sense and how to turn them down, I admire the honesty and directness displayed by Lord Orford when, in 1824, he was invited to become president of the Norwich Bible Society. He replied:

> Sir – I am surprised and annoyed by the contents of your letter – surprised, because my well-known character should have exempted me from such an application; and annoyed, because it compels me to have even this communication with you.
>
> I have long been addicted to the gaming table; I have lately taken to the turf; I fear I frequently blaspheme; but I have never distributed religious tracts. All this was known to you and your society, notwithstanding which you think me a fit person to be your president. God forgive your hypocrisy.
>
> I would rather live in the land of sinners than with such saints.

I have no idea how this wonderful letter fell into Samuel Butler's hands but he copied it into his notebooks. Yes, once in a while, it is best to come right out and say what you have to say, plainly and simply.

Thank-you letters

A response rather than a reply is also unquestionably necessary when you have been given hospitality or a present. People complain generally about a lack of 'pleases' and 'thank yous' in modern life, but what about that formalized communication, the written thank-you letter? Sometimes when I send presents off to my young relatives and friends, and the months go by without my hearing anything, I wonder whether these people have ceased to exist. Yet others describe a different experience. One woman wrote to me to say that the young friends to whom she dispensed gifts on birthdays and at Christmas were 'absolute angels' when it came to writing thank-you letters. It was their parents who had never yet thanked her for her wedding present who were the problem . . .

In writing thank-you letters it is important to remember that you are not on oath. You do not have to be completely honest about the level of enjoyment, or lack of it, you have experienced. In fact, a thank-you letter which attempts to indicate some degree of criticism or to hint at dissatisfaction will almost certainly fail in its purpose. Honesty is not the best policy with thank-you letters (unless you really did enjoy yourself) and white lies are the order of the day (as when thanking for a horrible gift, dinner or weekend). A confident blandness has to be adopted, I'm afraid, on all thanking occasions in order to make thanking easier on those occasions when it is not sincere.

It would be wrong ever to send a completely pro-forma thank-you letter. Each thank-you missive must be personalized to some extent – mentioning the gift, the food and your fellow guests, or some other detail specific to the occasion, in order to convey the particular pleasure that you are giving thanks for. Without being too embarrassing about it, a specific mention of how you are actually going to use a gift ('I'll be right out in the garden with it, just as soon as the bad weather clears') is always considered appropriate. In addition, this will remind the donors what on earth it was they gave you as well as convincing them that you have actually noticed what the gift was. You should also stress the generosity of the giver or host.

It is all a little irksome and a chore, writing thank-you letters, but if you can carry it off without making it seem either, then well done. A natural thank you is almost a contradiction in terms, but it is still worth striving after. In adult life, and in the wider world, an opinion poll survey revealed that about four in every ten people *never* actually write a thank you letter for a present, and almost seven out of every ten people *never* write to thank for a meal. There is no doubt that most people are very shaky, not to say inconsistent, on the subject of thank-you policy.

I am not inclined to be prescriptive on these questions of manners but surely, when it comes to thank yous, the rule is: when in doubt, do it. You can't really thank people *too much* – even though I do have a wonderful aunt, who when I write to thank her for something, automatically writes back to thank me for my thank-you. And so it goes on.

(Of a certain gentleman): His courtesy was somewhat extravagant. He would write and thank people who wrote to thank him for wedding presents and when he encountered anyone as punctilious as himself the correspondence ended only with death. – Evelyn Waugh in *Life Magazine*, 8 April 1946

The forcing of innocent young children to write thank-you letters does draw attention to the difference between manners which are motivated by doing the done thing and manners which spring from genuine feelings. It also raises uncomfortable questions about the way in which manners can be cunningly employed to advance your own interests. The bestower of the gift gives because it enables him or her to exercise some kind of hold over the recipient (even if only a momentary hold over the attention). The recipient may say thank you, not from real gratitude, but in order to ensure that the bestowal of gifts will continue.

A murky business, then, but one worth persevering with. Some people do have a *gift* for saying thank you, and to hear from them is really pleasurable. There are signs, too, that thanking is coming back into vogue. Sometimes staying for a weekend merits an immediate telephone call *and* a subsequent letter. If the speed of your written thanks is hastened by using the office franking machine, think again. The genuineness of your appreciation will be lessened by treating your kind hosts as a mere cog in the modern communication chain. Thanks by fax is never permitted, except among jokey friends. The fax message may be handwritten, which is good, but it is not the real thing.

I hesitate to recommend the first of these specimen thank-you letters but it is one way of reconciling a desire not to fib with the obligation to thank.

SPECIMEN LETTER 12: THANKING WITHOUT MEANING IT

The Cottage
Everly Drive
Surbiton
Surrey
KT1 2XY

Tel. 0X33-546109

2 March 199–

Dear Ian and Joan,

Just a line to say thank you for a most enjoyable evening. We were most interested to meet the Frasers at last, having heard so much about them. I hope we can all get together again very soon.

Our thanks again.

With best wishes,

Eric and Jane

Note, no mention is made of the fact that Mrs Fraser turned out to be a crashing bore or that Mr Fraser knocked a glass of wine over Jane's new trouser-suit. It was, after all, an enjoyable evening to the extent that nobody was sick afterwards, or indeed died. Yet, apart from the severe brevity of the note, it would be difficult to prise the sub-text from between the words as written. And that is only right.

Wedding present thank yous

It is only sensible to make sure that you know very clearly what present has come from whom. Keep labels attached. Write down the details. Then, when it is time to write thank-you letters, you can make them appropriate. To avoid the situation where you would have to spend the early, post-honeymoon weeks of your marriage writing thank-you letters, it is quite in order for you to start on this task before the wedding day. In other words, you can thank people for the presents before you are married. It makes sense for the couple to share the thank-you letter writing, according to who knows the sender best. This might be a very good moment to tell people what style the bride will wish to adopt following the marriage – 'Mrs Andrew Newly-Wed', 'Jennifer Single', 'Jennifer Single Newly-Wed', or whatever. That could save a lot of bother later on.

Try if possible to avoid formulaic phrases. People may feel sorry for you, having to write all these letters, but they are bound to recognize this kind of thing:

> Thank you ever so much for the lovely ——. Though we have eleven toast racks and three laundry baskets, until your —— arrived, we hadn't been given a single ——.

> It looks lovely against the grey walls of our sitting room and cheers us up whenever we look at it . . .

> It will always remind us of you . . .

SPECIMEN LETTER 13: THANKING FOR WEDDING PRESENT, BEFORE THE WEDDING

> The Cedars
> 235, Main Road
> Clutterby
> Staffordshire
> ST8 4ZZ

25 March 199–

Dear Richard and Catherine,

Thank you very much for the generous cheque that you have sent us. We can't tell you yet precisely what we are going to put it towards – but there are plenty of things on the list, we can assure you! When we know we will try and tell you.

It is lovely that you are both able to come to the wedding and we look forward to seeing you on the 15th. There is a lot of organizing to be done before then but Mummy is doing an amazing job in sorting everything out.

Until we see you, our thanks again,

With love,

June and Dominic

The address, as it happens, is that of the bride's parents. It is true that present-givers are said to want to know what their cheques have been spent on, but the promise to let them know is not meant very seriously. If present-givers really want to be remembered for something precise, they shouldn't give money presents.

SPECIMEN LETTER 14: THANKING FOR WEDDING PRESENT, AFTER THE WEDDING

2a, The Shore House

Saltings

Kent

KT3 4FF

Tel. 01XX-888999

Dear Susan and Geoffrey,

Thank you very much for the cheque. We have put it towards the inflatable dinghy we are going to get called a Tinker Tramp. The dinghy is very versatile as it converts to a life-raft or a sailing dinghy and it packs up very small, so it will be perfect for us.

Thank you for coming to the wedding two weeks ago. We had a lovely day. Mummy did an amazing job of organizing everything.

We had a wonderful honeymoon in Cornwall, even though the weather wasn't too good.

We look forward to welcoming you to our little flat if you are ever down this way.

Love from,

Christine and Alan

Christmas and birthday present thank yous

Few, if any, young people actually like writing thank-you letters – not least because presents may only have been given out of some misplaced obligation rather than genuine generosity. I can remember virtually copying out the same note to everyone when writing thank-yous for the umpteenth diary or box of handkerchiefs or postal order (in those days) sent at Christmas. There was the ritual hint of what I meant to spend the money on; the ritual mention of the trip to the pantomime (lots of exclamation marks); and the ritual concluding remark, 'Hope you are well'.

I look forward to the day when I can reasonably withhold presents from my young friends to save them the embarrassment and labour of having to write and thank me. Occasionally, the odd gem is produced, of course. Here now are two thank-you letters from small persons, who shall be nameless, as they are now both very grown up. They delight me still:

Dear Nigel,

Thank you very much for your card and three pound postal order. I am not sure what I am going to spend it on yet. I might get some more sweets or another book. But whatever I spend it on will be very useful. On Wednesday part of the playing field was under water.

I hope you are well,

Love . . .

dear Nigel Reece,

thank you for the book token I got a baby hamster and I called it happy when i hold it it bits my finger and I got three packits of soap and I got my birthday cake I blew the candles out in three blows the next saturday it was my party and we had my tape that I got from William. with love from Shirley xxxxxxxx

p.t.o. I would like to buy a ballet book.

SPECIMEN LETTER 15: RELEASE FROM THE CHORE OF HAVING TO WRITE THANK-YOU LETTERS

The Kirk House
56, Saxpence Avenue
Sporran
EDINBURGH
ED8 5YY

Tel. 076X-999999

17 August 199–

Dear Elizabeth,

I expect this may not reach you until after your birthday – for which, my apologies. I gather that you are having a good time and will probably be most reluctant to return and start earning your living from the law!

I thought I would give you the opportunity of being released from the awful responsibility – now that you *are* earning your living – of having to write thank-you letters for your Christmas and birthday presents. I know from my own experience what a chore it is, – and how faintly embarrassing it is for you to receive gifts of money at this time of your life. This does not, of course, preclude enormous and lavish presents being bestowed upon you on special occasions in the future.

I hope this does not seem too peculiar to you, and tell me if it does. We look forward to seeing you when you come to live in Edinburgh, as I presume you will.

With love from us both,

Kenneth

The interesting thing about this missive is that, although Elizabeth duly thanked Uncle Kenneth for his 'final' present, she gave no reaction in her thank-you letter to his courageous initiative. Ah well . . .

Party and dinner party thank yous

Some form of thank you is *always* necessary after you have accepted somebody's hospitality. But the nature of the thanks varies very much according to the occasion. Say you were invited to a birthday dinner or to a reasonably formal birthday party. You would presumably take some form of present, so it is not necessary to thank the host or organizer any further. Besides, if anyone needs thanking it is surely you – for having actually graced the occasion with your presence.

But a straightforward dinner party – even if you take a little gift for the host – still requires a thank-you message. In certain circumstances you might get away with a phone call the following day, but really it should be a written thank you.

As for a drinks party or a party where buffet refreshments are served, a thank you would not be necessary, unless you really want to say how much you have enjoyed yourself.

Theoretically, thank-you letters should be addressed to the *hostess* only, but given that parties and such tend to be paid for, if not actually arranged, by partners as well, I think this is a rule that may safely be ignored. Bear it in mind, though.

SPECIMEN LETTERS 16 & 17: THANK-YOU LETTERS AFTER
A DINNER PARTY

Flat 45a
Evelyn Mansions
Battersea
LONDON
SWX 3RR

Tel. 081-7X7 2001

3 December 199–

Dear Serena and Richard,

We did so enjoy ourselves last night. Thank you. Who were those marvellous Evans people? You certainly have some interesting friends!

We look forward to having you here soon.

With love from

Charles and Diana

There is nothing wrong with hints of ritual reciprocity – 'We look forward to having you here soon' – even if they may never come to anything. There is no harm, either, in going slightly over the top – however, I felt it was bit much of one of our guests to single out and swoon over my wife's *purée de betterave* (beetroot). It seemed quite comical. And too much of the 'delicious food, perfect company' sort of thing, begins to sound like advertising copy for a travel brochure.

The Mill House
Parsonage Road
Winterton
Norfolk
NN3 7PQ

Tel. 0X95-123987

Dear Geoffrey,

Belated thanks for a smashing evening. It was unusually agreeable to meet so many pleasant people at one time.

All best wishes to you and your spectacular lady from both of us.

Michael & Sparrow

Hospitality thank yous

If you go to stay with people, even if only for one night, you should write and thank them as soon as you can. Even if you don't feel they were put out by your visit – perhaps they didn't even cook you a meal, and let you share the breakfast they were having out of packets anyway – you should still do so. And even a one-night stay means that the bedding of the bed you slept in will have to be changed. For many hosts, too, simply having an unfamiliar body about the house can be a little draining, even if they do not put themselves out.

So a 'bread-and-butter' note is the order of the day. Never mind if it is going to be consigned instantly to the w.p.b. If you manage to compose something which is kept and treasured, then you have performed a miracle and are probably in line for the Nobel Prize for Literature.

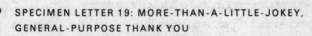

SPECIMEN LETTER 18: THANKING FOR HOSPITALITY

The Garden Flat
Christchurch Gardens
Chelsea
LONDON
SW3 4TU

Tel. 071-353 8X30

Dear Mrs Trevelyan,

I did so enjoy my weekend with you. It was a real treat for me to get out of London into the country – such a lovely part of the country, too – and a wonderful rest from my usual weekend chores. The Point-to-Point was great fun – it was the first time I had ever been to one.

The roads were surprisingly clear on the way back. Sebastian and I got to London in under an hour.

Again, thank you so very much.

Yours sincerely,

Selina

This is based on a sample letter in Sarah Maclean's *The Pan Book of Etiquette and Good Manners* (1962) – for a girl to write when she had been to stay with her boyfriend's parents. It is really rather touching in its complete innocuousness, lack of self-centredness and timeless applicability. And, yes, people do still write letters like that these days.

SPECIMEN LETTER 19: MORE-THAN-A-LITTLE-JOKEY,
GENERAL-PURPOSE THANK YOU

25, College Road
Bamforth
LEICESTER
Leicestershire
LE5 1TG

Tel. 08X45-784432

Dear Sam,

Just a line to say that, now the lights are dimmed and the shouting and the tumult have died down, what a rewarding and enriching experience it has been for us all to work with such a warm and real person as yourself, dedicated and entirely professional, yet truly reflecting that common touch which is the hallmark of the true artist and how privileged we have all been to have you grace our humble portals.

It is always sad when a job comes to an end, the team breaks up and the fond farewells have to be said but nonetheless the show must go on and what we have achieved together becomes just another milestone in the rich tapestry of mankind's puny endeavours to understand the meaning of life and the myriad patterns of nature and living things.

Yours ever,

John

I received something similar to this once. I laughed a lot.

Letters of sympathy

One of the hardest tasks is to write to an ill person and cheer them up without sounding mindlessly banal and without (if you know the illness is serious) being foolishly optimistic and hearty. This is why people usually tend to settle for the easy way out of a 'get well soon' card.

SPECIMEN LETTER 20: TO AN ILL PERSON

Cosy Towers
456, The Promenade
BOURNEMOUTH
Dorset
BH1 3DX

Tel. 0202-889X34

Dear Irene,

I was so sorry to hear from Ted that you had been taken so badly ill. You are such a one for putting on a brave face to the world that I had no idea quite how poorly you were. But I know that you have great reserves of strength and courage, so you will be in a good position to pull through and send all those doctors and nurses packing.

Just at the moment it is going to be difficult for me to come and see you in hospital but I will do my very best to get over soon.

Have a good rest – do what they tell you – and I'm sure you will soon be on the mend.

Good wishes and love from

Molly

Condolences

The writing and receiving of letters of condolence is one of the ways in which people can come to terms with the fact of death. To deny the bereaved this opportunity is to make matters that much harder to bear. Letters of condolence, though difficult to write – and to receive – are still wonderful things to have. It does not matter if they are awkwardly expressed or even very short.

Bernard Shaw found a gentle and almost humorous way of comforting Mrs Alfred Lyttelton when her husband of twenty-one years died in 1913. This is a paraphrase (which also dispenses with Shaw's idiosyncratic punctuation and grammar which he did not forbear to use even on an occasion like this):

So Alfred has stolen the march on us by a few years. I think he might have waited for you – but then, I suppose he couldn't exactly help himself on this occasion. We get our marching orders and off we have to go, leaving our wives and everything else behind us . . .

He will be at a loss without you for a while, just as you will be at a loss without him. But let me plead with you not to order any black things. Just rejoice in his memory and be radiant. Wear bright colours. Let others do the grieving for you . . .

Dying is a troublesome business: there is pain to be suffered, and it wrings one's heart; but death is a splendid thing – a warfare accomplished, a beginning all over again, a triumph. You can always see that in the faces of the dead, don't you think?

Be patient with the poor people who cry, especially the children. It is natural for them to do so. Cry yourself whenever you want to. Alfred is bound to be doing it, too, isn't he?

It is always best to write letters of condolence by hand. I have received a typewritten one (even with the typist reference number on, though with the 'Dear' line handwritten) and it almost took me longer to come to terms with that peculiar phenomenon than with the relative's death it was supposed to alleviate.

A minefield it can be, if you want it to be. But don't think about it. Just write what you feel, as spontaneously as you can. Be careful not to assume that the death was necessarily a 'blessed relief' – that may not be how it appears to the people most intimately involved. Similarly, avoid assumptions such as, 'perhaps one should look at his passing as being best for him'. The bereaved may have their own, better informed, view of such matters.

When are letters of condolence necessary? It rather depends on your closeness to the bereaved. On the whole, I think that if you are going to put in an appearance at the funeral, that should be enough. But you might well like to write something as well, as your presence at the funeral may not be remarked. Above all, letters of condolence are necessary whenever you think they can do some good. Don't be dissuaded from writing by the thought that you may only increase people's misery and unhappiness by drawing out the sadness. Usually, the reverse is the case. It is very comforting to receive letters – even from people who may not be very well known to you. Expressions of sympathy are just that – sympathetic to receive.

To whom should you address such letters? The relative or close friend of the deceased you know best. It is probably not wise to write to the widow of a dead man, if it is his daughter you know best. There is a good chance anyway that the children of the deceased will show any letters of condolence to the surviving parent, so your sympathy will find its way. And such things *may* count. I can recall an acquaintance of mine (then in his twenties) complaining that none of his contemporaries had written to him when his mother died. He was right to complain, but I am not completely surprised that the friends hadn't rallied round in the way he expected.

What language should you use? Does it have to be euphemistic? Well, no, it doesn't. If you want to say, 'I was so sorry to hear that your mother had died', then say it. Just consider what the receiver of your letter might want. If that person wishes to be cushioned by euphemisms, who is to deny him or her the pleasure? In time of mourning, clichés don't matter – in fact, there is comfort in them. They are the currency of condolences and are not to be despised: 'She will be very greatly missed by so many people. . . . He was one of nature's gentlemen. . . . He was a big man in every way. . . . Yours with deepest sympathy . . .'. At the very first funeral I attended (of a much-loved great-uncle), one of his friends said to me, 'Another page turned in the Book of Life . . .' and I have never questioned anybody's right to say that sort of thing since.

Don't send a condolence card – that is to say, a pre-printed one, even though this may help you bypass the difficulties outlined above. Say what you have to say, in your own words.

SPECIMEN LETTER 21: TO A BEREAVED PERSON FROM AN ACQUAINTANCE

> 34, Goddard Way
> Blundson
> **SWINDON**
> Wiltshire
>
> Tel. 0793-X78899
>
> 11 June 199–
>
> My dear Amy,
>
> I write to say how sad I was to hear that your mother had died and to offer condolences to you and your family, both from myself and my wife. I had come to know Emma quite well in recent years and very much appreciated her kind interest. She served our community in so many ways and we shall all miss her very much.
>
> You are in our thoughts and in our prayers.
>
> Yours very sincerely,
>
> Jim

**SPECIMEN LETTER 22: TO A BEREAVED PERSON FROM
A RELATIVE (NOT CLOSE) – EXCERPT**

. . . I remember her with great affection and for the kindness she
showed me over the last few years. I am sorry that I cannot attend
the funeral but family commitments and illness make it impossible,
but nevertheless my thoughts will be with you at this sad time.

**SPECIMEN LETTER 23: TO A BEREAVED PERSON FROM
A RELATIVE (QUITE CLOSE) – EXCERPT**

. . . Alison and I send you our deep sympathy on the loss of your
mother. It is sad that her health deteriorated so suddenly, but she
has been spared much suffering and anxiety. Perhaps, Margaret,
one should look at her passing as being best for her.

With love to you and to Raymond . . .

Again, it is wise to be cautious when making the sort of assumptions
contained in this letter, even if they are fairly commonplace. Not
everyone will agree that death was the best thing that could have
happened to someone, so tread carefully.

Acknowledging sympathy letters

Try not to respond with a formal printed card, if you can help it, though
this might be appropriate in the case of illness. You might simply be too
weak to write very much. After a death, always write in your own hand.
Although it appears customary for families that have received anything
more than a few letters of condolence to have formal cards of acknowledgement printed, my own view is that a brief handwritten letter of
thanks is still preferable. Never mind if writing many such notes takes a
long time to do. It is unlikely that it will make the burden of loss any
worse, and may even help lighten it.

Another method is to place a notice in the local newspaper:

The family of the late Mrs —— —— wish to thank all relatives and
friends for the kind expressions of sympathy they received during
their recent bereavement.

But not everyone who wrote will see this thank you. The fact remains that a personal letter of thanks, however short, is wonderful to receive and curiously satisfying to send.

SPECIMEN LETTER 24: ACKNOWLEDGING A LETTER OF SYMPATHY (i)

> Grampian House
> Foveran Street
> Aberdeen
> Grampian
> AB4 0XF

6 May 199–

Dear Tom,

You have written just when your thoughts were most appreciated.

Bless you, and thank you, from both me and the girls.

With love from
Dora

P.S. Can we all see you in a week or two? I would love to have your advice about what to do next.

SPECIMEN LETTER 25: ACKNOWLEDGING A LETTER OF SYMPATHY (ii)

> 23, Clarence Crescent
> Old Portsmouth
> Hampshire
> PO1 3CV

Tel. 0705-XX756912

15 December 199–

Dear George and Margaret,

Please forgive me for taking so long to thank you for the letter you sent when Mary died, but only now do I feel I can cope with writing.

I have had so many cards and letters, they have been such a help and comfort to me. It was very kind of you to write.

With best wishes,

Peter

Apologies

It takes a great deal of courage and humanity to write a letter of apology, but it is worth doing. The size of the original offence will be reduced to insignificance by a handsome letter of apology.

 SPECIMEN LETTER 26: APOLOGIZING

The Dog House
Oakfordbridge Terrace
TIVERTON
Devon
EX16 8QW

Tel. (0884) 40X56

5 January 199–

Dear Tim,

I am writing to say how sorry I am for what happened last night. It was completely unforgivable to have behaved like that at your dinner table and to have caused you any embarrassment at all when we were all supposed to be enjoying ourselves.

I don't know what got into me and I very much hope that you will forgive me. Even more so, I hope that Eleanor and yourself will forget that the incident ever took place. I value your friendship too much to hope otherwise.

With all good wishes,

Yours sincerely,

Guy

Were this letter to be accompanied by flowers for Eleanor, so much the better.

Reading other people's letters

There is an old English proverb, 'Neither eyes on letters nor hands in coffers', which neatly equates reading other people's correspondence with stealing. Of course it is tempting to look at other people's letters, just as it is to pry into their diaries, because by doing so we get the feeling that we are seeing into their thoughts in a way that might otherwise be denied to us. The popularity of published letters is another indication of this particular form of privacy invasion.

Reading other people's letters is like eavesdropping on their spoken conversations, however, and can no more be condoned than that activity. Other people's letters should not be read uninvited. The correspondence of dead people is a slightly different matter. That they have not destroyed the letters themselves – or given instructions for this – may be taken as permitting inspection. But this is a murky area. Old letters can be wonderful historical source material and the many literary disputes that have broken out over the possession and publication of letters is testimony to the sensitivities involved.

Accordingly, it is always good practice to assume that the privacy of letter is never one hundred per cent assured, and to write with an appropriate measure of circumspection. Talleyrand, the French statesman, had a servant to whom he entrusted a letter for delivery. Looking out of the window, he observed the man reading the letter. On the following day, Talleyrand gave the servant another letter to deliver, this time with the postscript: 'You may send a verbal answer by the bearer. He is perfectly acquainted with the whole business, having taken the precaution of reading this prior to its delivery.'

∾ 7 ∾

TAKE A LETTER,
MS SMITH

Now it is time to take a look at business and professional letters – not only within and from business but to business. In other words, letters whether the writer is on the inside or the outside of an organization or company. In both cases, slightly different rules apply to those that obtain in social and personal correspondence. Any letter dealing with non-social and non-personal matters obviously requires a different tone of voice, a different style and more formal accompaniments. But it is my belief that business correspondence would benefit from even more loosening up of its formal traditions and from an increasingly personal tone (in the best sense of that word). However contemporary some business letters may now sound, it is surprising how easily people writing them slip back into the bad old formal ways.

'They [letters] are the soul of trade.' – James Howell (1594?-1666), *Touching the Vertu and Use of Familiar Letters*, line 41

'I find by experience that it is much more rational, as well as easy, to answer a letter of real business by the return of the post.' – Edward Gibbon in a letter to Lord Sheffield (9 September 1789)

'Businessmen aren't writers, your honour. There's only one businessman in a thousand that can write a good letter of recommendation.' – Thornton Wilder, *The Matchmaker* (1954)

The fustian of business correspondence – such dated phrases as 'yours to hand', 're yours of the 5th ult', 'we are in receipt of your communication' 'thanking you in kind anticipation of your reply' 'thank you for your time and consideration' – are taking a curiously long time to die out. When people get into business letter writing mode, they seem to reach back to these old dinosaur formulae because they think this is what is required of them. I suppose they feel, too, that there is a safety to be had from the traditional phrases.

Letterspeak

All 'letterspeak' is to be avoided, however, and this applies not only to phrases like 're yours of the 5th ult' (which no one in their right minds would ever have 'said', anyway) but also to the pompous, polysyllabic meanderings that people so easily slip into. If you wouldn't say 'with regard to' in conversation, you shouldn't put it in a letter either. Even 'regarding' is a word that smells of the quill pen and the Dickensian desk, when you can say 'about' just as well. Short words are the best and conversational ones all the more so.

If you mean, 'please deliver as soon as possible', then say so. Don't put 'it would be of the greatest assistance if the delivery was effected at your earliest convenience . . .'. As for 'assuring you of our best attentions at all times . . .', leave that to the Head of Grovelling. Groucho Marx once seized on a cliché of business correspondence which a bank manager unthinkingly appended – the one about 'If I can be of service to you, please do not hesitate to call on me . . .'. Marx immediately wrote back: 'Dear Sir, The best thing you can do to be of service to me is to steal some money from the account of one of your richer clients and credit it to mine.'

This said – and while still encouraging you to use the simplest and most straightforward language you can think of – there are some basic and sensible rules you should always think about before writing and sending off a business letter.

The only really important thing to be encouraged in business correspondence is that employees and the outsiders they are dealing with remember to put any *reference number* or designation that will enable the company or organization to deal with a letter swiftly.

It is also important that company signatories should put their own *name* clearly, together with some indication of what position they hold within the company or organization. No outsider feels confident that a letter addressed to 'ICI' or 'The BBC' will easily find its way to the right target, so a more precise and individual addressee needs to be indicated.

Similarly, signing off simply with 'Walker & Co.' or 'For and on behalf of . . .' may help to shift liability on to the company, but it does not make customers or clients feel warmly towards it. A letter is a personal communication. Companies and organizations are incapable of grasping a fountain pen and should not make that pretence.

In fact, there is much to be said for using the 'I' rather than the royal 'we' form in all business communications. It puts responsibility on a clearly identifiable individual and not on some vaguely defined company ethos.

A simple *signature* should always be accompanied by a typed form of the name to enable it to be deciphered, followed by the signer's job title. The source of the letter will be indicated by the name of the company or organization on the letterhead; the individual responsible for the letter will be clear from the signer's name and designation.

It is also vital that writers should keep *copies* of any correspondence so that they can recall what they have said, and when it was written and posted. Casualness in these matters is just not appropriate in business correspondence, even if it can sometimes be allowed in social and personal communication.

Political correctness

This is a comparatively recent term for an obsessive, over-zealous and insidious approach to language. Its aim is to weed out racist, sexist and other words likely to offend various minorities. You don't have to subscribe to PC in order to realize that lack of sensitivity in the words you use is foolish in any form of correspondence. In dealing with the public at large, however, not to think about the problem is simply bad for business.

A basic example of unthinking letter writing would be for a hotel manager to confirm a room reservation for two people and then say, 'We look forward to welcoming you and your wife to the Antrobus Hotel . . .'. The days are long gone when hotels required the 'Mr and Mrs Smith' act on behalf of unmarried couples. They should now not make the slightest assumption about the people who are paying to stay with them. They should acknowledge the booking of a double-bedded room 'for the night of . . .' and speculate no further.

The aim should always be to write to a customer or client using language that will not alienate him or her. It may be difficult, but the aim should be to anticipate what the customer or client is likely to find acceptable in the way of words – and to select those words only. At the simplest level, never mind the perils of using ageist or sexist language, or expressing such points of view – it obviously makes sense to treat the target of your letter as a human being who may have strong views on any number of matters. Tread carefully, in other words. Listen carefully. Anticipate. Be sensitive.

Messrs and Ltd

At one time it was considered incorrect to put both 'Messrs' and 'Ltd' on the same envelope. However, 'Messrs' (plural of 'Mr' and an abbreviation of the French *messieurs*) has now almost completely disappeared from use, and a limited company is now quite likely to be a public limited company (written 'plc' or 'PLC'), anyway.

Is there an expectation that all business correspondence be typed? Yes. For ease of reading, clarity of display, and air of seriousness, there is no beating a typewritten letter. However, handwritten personal notes and handwritten emendations to typed text certainly have a place and help to humanize business correspondence.

So now let's begin by looking at correspondence *within* business as opposed to correspondence coming from outside customers and clients (which will be dealt with in the next chapter). It can be said that letter writing is one of the most powerful business tools available to you. Word power is a cheap resource but you have to use it with care. You are probably better at letter writing than you think, so learn to use your strengths in communication. Keep your ears and eyes open for examples of effective communication and apply the lessons you learn to effective letter writing.

An example of the basic business letter:

SPECIMEN LETTER 27: BUSINESS GENERAL

WORDS ARE OUR BUSINESS LTD

Unit 286, Shakespeare Business Park, Bard Street,
Stratford-upon-Avon, Warwickshire SL1 7PT
Tel. 0789-4556X456 Fax. 0789-8888X452

Charles Dickens
Bleak House
BROADSTAIRS
Kent
CT1 D23   23 February 199–

Dear Mr Dickens,

Agreement no. 23577864

I am happy to tell you that this agreement has now been put into immediate effect. I will send you your copy as soon as it comes back from the legal department.

With good wishes,

Yours sincerely,

Amanda Toady
Customer Services Assistant

AT/23

There you are – not great literature, but no messing about and no clichés. Knowing that Mr Dickens is a bit of a crusty old sort, Amanda might well have been advised to put Miss/Mrs or Ms before or after her own name (to help Mr Dickens in his dealings with her: from what we know of him, he seems unlikely to wish to call her 'Amanda'). The 'AT/ 23' is the typist's code, meaning that typist no. 23 typed a letter originated by AT, Amanda Toady.

Acknowledgements

However laborious it may seem, a simple letter – or, rather, postcard – of acknowledgement is mandatory if a company or organization is unable or unlikely to be able to respond fully to an outside query within two or three days. Otherwise, customers or clients feel that their letters have disappeared into a deep void.

SPECIMEN LETTER 28: STANDARD ACKNOWLEDGEMENT

WORDS ARE OUR BUSINESS LTD

Unit 286, Shakespeare Business Park, Bard Street,
Stratford-upon-Avon, Warwickshire SL1 7PT
Tel. 0789-4556X456 Extension 234 Fax. 0789-8888X452

Ref. GHB/2234

Thank you for your letter of . . . . which is receiving attention.
We hope to let you have a reply very shortly.

Yours sincerely,

[Initials or signature + *legible* name and job title of the
acknowledger]

The name and address of the addressee do not need to be repeated on
the message side of the postcard. Nor is it necessary for the sender to
resort to 'Dear Sir/Madam' or any of that sort of thing. Again, as I show,
it is important for whoever signs the card on behalf of the company to
make his or her identity apparent. This enables the sender to pursue the
matter more easily should no fuller reply actually materialize.

A pox on by proxy

How should one feel if one receives a typed letter signed not by the
sender but 'p.p.', the sender's secretary? It stands for *per procurationem*,
which is Latin for 'by proxy', not 'on behalf of', and so, in theory, it
should precede the secretary's name rather than that of the person the
letter is being sent on behalf of.

I think it is a wretched practice. It quite often appears to be used
even when the dictator of the letter is still around the office and quite
capable of signing it. I suppose if waiting for the dictator's own
signature meant that a letter was unduly delayed, there might be
something to be said for 'p.p.', but it is pretty ungracious even so.
Putting 'Dictated by —— —— and signed in his absence' is similarly
all very elaborate and unlikeable.

Once I received a letter of congratulation about something signed 'p.p.' by the sender's secretary, thus completely negating any kindness of thought, and indeed demolishing any reciprocal feelings on my part.

Just think of the potential influence you hold over a client or customer by signing your own name yourself. The personal touch is all important. If you yourself sign a letter, then you yourself have personally touched the notepaper. It is foolish in the extreme to let any minor person intervene between you and success. It's as simple as that.

Post power

Is dictation the cause of all ills in business correspondence? It certainly has a lot to do with it. Dictating into a machine is like giving an off-the-cuff speech – it is impossible to do well without recourse to ready-formed bits of junk language that rumble out of your memory. And because dictators do not see the shape of the letter building up before their eyes, they are unable to impose any real order or shape on their material. Dictators think in a straight line, often only realizing what they have said (if then) when they have reached the end of a long sentence.

It takes a legal brain – the kind which somehow enables the speaker almost to see the points on an invisible screen at the front of the brain – to dictate sensibly. Until the day when dictation becomes redundant – that is to say, the day when people prepare all their own letters on a word processor and secretaries are put out to grass – there are one or two ways in which the end product may be improved.

The dictator should 'engage brain before opening mouth' – in other words, *think* about the letter before starting to formulate a reply to it. Possibly jot down a framework and key points and phrases. Above all, have the letter which is being replied to in easy reach as the dictation is being carried out.

The write stuff

I was once told of the businessman who bustled into a design studio and announced that he was intent on having a 'lurgi' for his corporate stationery. This only goes to show how the importance of having a good visual corporate image, complete with a sympathetic logo, has penetrated into most areas of business these days.

The transformation that has overtaken company letterheads and envelopes, indeed corporate design generally, in recent years is marked indeed. Many companies and organizations now realize the importance of training staff how to use the telephone, and appreciate that an efficient switchboard is vital not only to give an initial good impression to potential customers but as the chief conduit of business to the company. Similarly, stationery is seen as expressing a good corporate image and the content of letters is not just considered a luxury that is only right if left to chance.

Business stationery is probably best put out to a designer who will ensure that it becomes part of a wider strategy to present a good image. Nevertheless, it should contain certain basic information: name of the business, address, telephone and fax numbers (and relevant extensions to speed callers on their way through), the company's registered office address (if this is different to the business address), the company registration number, and names of the directors.

Incoming mail

Incoming mail should be stamped with date and time, just in case any dispute arises as to when a particular piece of mail actually arrived. It should be distributed to the addressee as quickly as humanly possible. Outgoing mail should be dealt with equally speedily. Aiming to reply to all letters by return of post is no bad aim for anybody, but especially for a business.

All letters received, of whatever kind, should be filed and kept for an agreed period. Weeding out for space reasons is a time-consuming process which may safely be put off for years. Usually, after a reasonable period, it will be obvious which letters can be destroyed.

The British field marshal who became 1st Earl Alexander (d. 1969) had the habit, at the end of the working day, of tipping whatever remained in his In tray into his Out tray. When asked why he did this, he replied, 'Because it saves time. You'd be surprised how little of it comes back.'

Personal mail and the office

It is not good business practice for employees to be allowed to use corporate notepaper for their private purposes. An employee's personal correspondence should be conducted from home and not seek to obtain any kudos from being under the false auspices of a big organization. It is also bad form, from a social point of view, if an employee uses corporate notepaper (and stamp franking) for personal letters. Company letterheads and such should *never* be used for personal notes, thank yous and the rest.

By hand

If a letter is being hand delivered, it is customary to put 'By hand' or 'By courier' or 'By taxi' in the right hand corner of the envelope where the postage stamps would have been. This helps to explain how the missive managed to be delivered so quickly or why it did not arrive with the rest of the mail.

Memo to memo-writers

A memorandum is, if you like, an internal letter. The quality of memos would no doubt be improved if as much care went into their preparation as it does into outwardly directed letters. I once worked under a memo-holic who flooded the office with his thoughts and instructions on an almost hourly basis. There is something to be said for 'getting things down on paper' – where they can be referred to – but this form of verbal diarrhoea was an indication of his shortcomings in staff management. He was obsessed with the detail of office administration. He was unable to talk to people directly about matters which obsessed him. (When he retired, we presented him with his *Complete Memoranda* – bound, and running to several volumes.)

Added to the old-fashioned memo hazard, we now have electronic mail within the office (which may or may not be backed up with paper copies) or computerized desk-to-desk mail, however you like to think of it.

In the efficient office, memos are kept to a minimum and are treated as though they were actual letters. That is to say, they are given as much thought as formal letters and copies of them are kept.

Dealing with complaints

Writing a letter of complaint to a company costs no money to speak of. All it costs is blood, sweat and tears. The complainant's anger will carry him or her through. But for the company or organization to deal with that complaint – well, that can be a very costly process indeed. Answering business complaints, or simply responding to the views of customers or to people asking for information about products and services, is no small item in a company's budget. Most large organizations now have departments which deal with mail coming from outside.

Unfortunately the rise in consumerism has been met by a matching rise in the number of paid obfuscators. It would be hard to put a percentage on the amount of correspondence a company or organization receives which is time-wasting, mischief-making, or just plain barmy. But any company or organization needs to think deeply about how it responds to genuine criticism and complaint from outside.

The wrong way to go about it is for a company or organization to be patronizing: 'I have been handed your letter and asked to reply to it, and to let you know that your comments have been noted and will be drawn to the attention of those directly concerned . . .' It is even worse if this sort of waffle is sent after a considerable amount of time has elapsed. It is absolutely insulting – and very bad for any organization's image – if the recipients of any official response are given to believe that they are merely receiving a standard reply.

There is an old story (told for example in *Pass the Port*, 1976) of the distinguished gentleman – an ambassador, no less – who had an unfortunate experience when travelling. He was bitten by bugs. Duly complaining to the travel company, he received a fulsome letter of apology back – 'unhappily, the clerk who dealt with the complaint, by inadvertence, attached to this reply the Ambassador's original letter of complaint, across which someone had scribbled, "Usual bug letter, please".'

Any benefit to be derived from sending a pro-forma apology is, of course, completely negated if there is proof or suspicion that it is not genuine. Another version of the above story – which must have a grain of truth in it – is that a woman who had complained also chanced to see the instruction, 'Send the old bat the standard two Kleenex reply . . .'.

Of course, it is impossible for companies to reply quickly and easily to letters requiring detailed factual replies, just as it is very difficult for a government department, say, to rustle up the sort of replies which – when asked in parliament – cost thousands of pounds to research. The first step is to issue an acknowledgement speedily. The next best move is for the person to whom the original letter was addressed to retain the responsibility of answering it. That applies to the company chairman as much as to anyone else lower down the hierarchy.

There are few things more impressive than a reply coming direct from the person to whom a query or complaint was originally directed. And that means the reply signed by that person and not 'p.p.' any minion either. Complaint handling and letter answering can say a lot about how an organization is run, as also about its confidence in itself and morale within it.

SPECIMEN LETTER 29: RESPONSE TO A COMPLAINT (CONTAINED IN SPECIMEN LETTER 48)

FROM THE CHAIRMAN OF SPAGHETTI COMPUTERS PLC.
Elephant House, Fulham Broadway, London SW6 7FF
Tel. 071-X54 2000 Fax. 071-X54 3030

Adrian Hack
Managing Director
Cottage Industry Ltd
Sunrise Valley
Carshalton
Surrey
KT3 4RR   9 February 199–

Dear Mr Hack,

I was very concerned yesterday to receive your letter dated 8th February and to learn that our response to your service needs has disappointed you. You are quite right to point out how we encourage our customers to rely so heavily upon our service staff and it is obviously most unsatisfactory if they fail to meet their response targets.

This morning I spoke to —— ——, who is in charge of servicing for your area and he will ring you tomorrow to explain the most unfortunate clutch of circumstances which caused us to disappoint you. Should you not have heard from —— —— by the end of tommorow, please ring my number and tell me.

I know that nothing can make up for the frustration and lost time that you have suffered but you can count on us to make sure that it will not happen again.

Yours very truly,

Luigi Jones

LJ/erh

This did not entirely soothe Mr Hack, who was so annoyed he would probably only have been calmed down by being bathed in warm asses' milk and given a tea chest full of thousand-pound notes. But the chairman's response was personal and rapid (it was even faxed as well as sent by post). The chairman also provided Mr Hack with a useful direct line in case of further mishaps. For sound business reasons he did not start offering compensation.

The moral is that standard letters and acknowledgements produce a standard response in those to whom they are addressed – they are not popular. So . . .

Beware standard replies

The regimented, standard reply probably originated, with good reason, in wartime, when mail from members of the services is customarily subjected to censorship. An extreme example of the type, known as a 'Field Service Post Card' was issued during the First World War:

NOTHING is to be written on this side except the date and signature of the sender. Sentences not required may be erased. If anything else is added the post card will be destroyed.

_____

I am quite well.
I have been admitted into hospital.
    (sick   ) and am going on well.
    (wounded   ) and hope to be discharged soon.
I am being sent down to the base.

I have received your   (letter dated _____)
                         (telegram _____)
                         (parcel _____)

Letter follows at first opportunity.
I have received no letter from you
                  (lately)
                  (for a long time)*

Signature only

Date _____

Pretty dismal, eh? Standard communications are never a good thing, whatever effort they may save. Every letter written to *Blue Peter*, BBC Television's long-running children's show, receives an *individual* reply. The reason for this, according to Biddy Baxter, the programme's editor from 1962-88, was because of Enid Blyton, the famous children's author. As a six-year-old, Baxter wrote two fan letters to Blyton. The first letter, a hymn of praise, received a wonderful reply from the author, 'very chatty and with her own address on the top – I felt she was writing to me. But, being a typical child, I wrote again three days later. I got back exactly the same letter. I remembered for ever how awful I felt that day.'

(This salutary experience was recounted in *Kingsgate*, Durham University's alumni magazine, September 1992.)

With compliments

There is a lot to be said for *not* writing business letters, if you can possibly avoid it. Dictating, typing and sending off a letter is something that can be costed out quite simply. It might surprise you just how expensive it actually is to put in a covering letter which simply says, 'Please look at the document that you will also find in the envelope.'

In other words, consider whether a simple compliments slip will do the job of a full-blown letter. If it shows the name of your company or organization and it is quite obvious who is sending the material, then choose the simpler method. It is also friendlier.

References and Referees

The business of seeking references, writing references and following up references is an important part of all business and professional life. In the academic world, to take but one example, it often threatens to take up valuable time which could be spent teaching or studying, but nevertheless it has to be done.

If you need to supply the names and addresses of referees, say for a job application, it is – naturally – only polite that the permission of these people be sought before their names are given. It may be that the references will not actually be taken up and they will not be put to any trouble. But writing references is a demanding business and you are hardly likely to get a good one from someone whose cooperation you have assumed.

So, much better to *write* to the potential referee and say what it is all about.

 SPECIMEN LETTER 30: ASKING SOMEONE TO BE A REFEREE

89, Woodstock Avenue

Worple Heath

Surrey

SU8 5XT

Tel. 01X6-675849

28 October 199–

Dear Mr Robinson,

You will remember that when we met last month at the I Zingari football match, I mentioned to you that I was intending to leave my job at Science Profile PLC and move into manufacturing.

Rather more quickly than I expected, I have come across an opportunity with Mountain Trailers – on the research and development side – in Brecon. They have asked me to supply them with the names of two referees, one of whom must have known me in a working capacity.

I would most appreciate it if you would be my 'work' referee. Please can you let me know whether you would be willing to do this for me, so that I can put your name and address on the application forms? I hope this will not cause you too much trouble.

With many thanks, in anticipation,

Yours sincerely,

Steven McGraw

P.S. I shall, of course, let you know how I get on.

This last point is very important. It is a basic courtesy to keep the referee informed of your progress and to let the person know the outcome of your application, even if it comes to nothing.

Should Steve McGraw enclose an S.A.E. when writing to Mr Robinson? Yes, as he specifically requests an indication from Robinson whether he is prepared to provide a reference or not. Enclosing an S.A.E. would certainly not do any harm but, given that Mr Robinson will probably be writing under the auspices of a company, it is not strictly necessary.

It would be most unusual for anyone taking up references not to do so themselves. Usually, they would not expect the applicant to procure and pass on a referee's letter. This way, the applicant does not actually get to see what is being written about him or her. This may make it easier for the referee to be candid.

At the general level, it can be embarrassing to be asked to speak up for someone who is undeserving of a 'good' reference, particularly if what you write is likely to be seen by that person. If you have any doubts, you should excuse yourself with some such statement as, 'I make it a rule not to – it's nothing personal', even though this may not get you off the hook with some persistent people.

If you do have to go through with it, then it is most important to say in your letter only what you believe to be true. After all, you might find yourself in a court of law if you don't. Rather than trying to communicate your true feelings (if they are unfavourable, that is) by coded hints, it is safer simply to be brief and say only what you can say sincerely – in other words, that which is truthful. Praise what you think is worth praising about a person's character or performance. Hope that the receiver of the reference will read between your lines and deduce from whatever you leave out that those are the areas where the candidate may be wanting. It is best not to *volunteer* information that you consider the person dishonest, for example. If this is an important question for future employers, they can always 'take up the reference' and ask you the question direct.

Similar considerations apply when friends and acquaintances write to you for work for themselves, or when they ask you to find a job for their offspring. If you are happy to oblige, well and good, but if you genuinely can't help, or do not wish to, make it clear that company policy is that recruitment is by group decision and not by you individually. Try not to give precise reasons for turning down applicants, as this may lead to prolonged arguments. 'We do not have an opening *at this time'* is a well-worn phrase of rejection because it is suitably vague and does not suggest that there is anything wrong with the particular candidate.

SPECIMEN LETTER 31: PROVIDING A REFERENCE

Pasta House
Southern Business Park
Greenwich
LONDON
PP1 8SS

Tel. 09X6-678493 Ext. 2456

Sheila Bean
Personnel Director
Mountain Trailers Ltd
Utopia Factory
BRECON
XX1 1YY

14 November 199–

Dear Sheila Bean,

Steven McGraw – job no. Rg235B

Thank you for your letter of 8 November asking for my views on Steven McGraw. I was expecting it, of course.

I have known Steven for about eight years now since he came to work for us straight from university as a junior scientific officer. He settled into his working life a good deal more confidently than some I have known and was always never less than competent. He was personally always very affable and had the respect of his colleagues.

Unfortunately, as with so many first jobs, he discovered rather too late that he was not cut out for working in a medium-sized organization where he had to be more self-directed than he was ready for. He then went on to Science Profile where I think he may have done better, although my contacts with him have only been occasional since he left this company.

I gather that he would now like to move right out of research and put his scientific skills to use in manufacturing. This strikes me as being a positive step and it is one that I am actively encouraging him in. I think his particular talents are more for science applications. It is possible, too, that his personality will come through rather better in a manufacturing or marketing role. He had a sad personal misfortune just after he left us – the girl he was going to marry was killed in a car accident – but I expect he has sorted himself out by this time.

I can thoroughly recommend Steven in a general sense. He is honest, hard-working, direct and affable, and I hope that he may find the job he requires with you. Do please call me or write if you would like amplification of this or any further details.

With best wishes,

Yours sincerely,

Arthur Robinson

If Steven McGraw ever got to see this letter, I think he would think it a very positive recommendation. It is not over-effusive but cautious, and may be all the more effective for that reason. It is apparent from the steady tone that Arthur Robinson quite likes the lad and hopes we will get the job, but the tone signals to the potential employers that they will have to do some thinking and investigating of their own. The inclusion of the personal detail about the fiancée's death is a useful one. It is unlikely that Steven would have volunteered the information himself at any stage to his future employer but it might provide an important piece in the jigsaw. Robinson's letter is also open in tone. He does not appear to be holding anything back or signalling that he is *not* mentioning anything important. His last paragraph shows that he is willing to help further if necessary.

There are occasions when a reference is vital in filling in the background – even the foreground – to a subject's personality. Perhaps the applicant is poor at interviews. Here the whole point of the reference is to reflect what the subject is like when not going through the artificial rigours of interviewing and assessment.

Such references may make all the difference between success and failure, for example, when a bright person consistently falls down in

examinations or other types of test. Schoolteachers can perform miracles
of life-saving by carefully worded but revealing personal assessments.
Their pupils' lives and futures are in their hands. Here, based on an
actual letter, is a headmaster going into bat (successfully as it turned
out) for a sixth former wishing to go to one of the older universities:

 SPECIMEN LETTER 32: A PERSONAL RECOMMENDATION

> From: The Headmaster,
> The Old School,
> Beddows,
> Essex,
> HA3 5XT

5 September 199–

. . . W.P. is a pupil of unusual promise and interest. . . . His work is
characterized by intellectual grasp rather than obvious imaginative
gift. His claim for distinction rests on the ability and interest which
he has shown in a number of enterprises outside the classroom. . . .
W.P. has a modest and unassuming personality. He is well balanced
with nothing of the exhibitionist in his make-up. He is always ready
to spend time and effort on activities for the benefit of the
school. . . . He might well have a distinguished career in the field
which he has chosen. His family background is a good one. . . .

W.P. is a pleasant fellow with a developed sense of humour. He
combines a sensitive and introspective disposition with genuine
public spirit. Absorption in his interests and hobbies has not
prevented him from doing considerable work for the benefit of
the school. He has made a good and reliable school prefect and
contributed in many ways to the community life of the school. He
has the respect of his contemporaries . . .

There is no place for coded qualification here. Such letters are designed
to 'sell, sell, sell'. As I say, there are circumstances in which everything
depends on them.

'Selling' letters and mail-shots

As for 'selling' letters in the more obviously commercial sphere – well, a good deal may depend on them, too, though I wonder just how well thought out most of them are. The whole idea of what purports to be a personal letter – with the recipient's name and address and a computer-customized 'Dear Mr XYZ . . .' at the start – is questionable. Nobody is fooled into mistaking this for anything other than the advertising mail-shot that it actually is.

As for the 'letters' which follow, they are almost invariably written in leaden prose, unpersuasive language, and are, without exception, *far too long* – thus breaking the number one golden rule of this book. It is not unusual for you to receive four-page letters from the Consumers' Association, for example, with lots of underlinings and odd lines printed in different colours, inviting you to subscribe to *Which?* or buy *The Good Food Guide*. Or letters from the bank offering you health care (which come in an envelope full of leaflets and forms of several different sizes, just like confetti).

No doubt the perpetrators of these monstrosities will claim that 'market research has shown that people like receiving information about new products, etc. etc.'. They can probably prove that some people do actually wade through all the wordage, but I very much doubt it. Any screed of obvious advertising material – particularly when over one page in length – is a prime candidate for the dustbin, unread.

'Selling letters' with their fake personalization and printed-on signatures from the sender degrade the whole process of letter writing. By seeming to attract, they merely disappoint. There are few worse starts to the day than finding that what has plopped through your letter box with a healthy sound is not a bundle of real letters but another serving of advertising rubbish. The perpertrators of mail-shots calculate that it is a worthwhile activity even though the 'take-up' rate is only about 1 per cent. This is a pitifully small response, particularly when it means that 99 per cent of the stuff they shovel out is going to be put out as waste. Funnily enough, it always seems to be the 99 per cent rubbish that gets put through *your* letter box . . .

Testimonials

When businesses and organizations receive letters of commendation and appreciation, are they entitled to use them for promotional purposes? Leaving aside the question of whether anybody is going to be impressed by whatever 'Mr T.E. Jones of Newport' has to say about his new carpet sweeper – wouldn't most people assume that either his is a made-up name or that he has somehow been persuaded to endorse the product? – the answer is yes. Testimonials are a traditional way of promoting products and services. Their roots may be found in the commendatory poems and prefaces that used to clutter the front of books in Shakespeare's day. Much early advertising was based on quoting things said about the product by allegedly satisfied users.

The provider of an endorsement must, however, be formally consulted and asked for permission. This applies equally to unknown members of the public as to well-known names.

In the United States, where this sort of thing is much more understood (and more readily responded to), the whole process is organized along traditional lines:

SPECIMEN LETTER 33: SEEKING A TESTIMONIAL

Dear Mr . . .

[The writer explains who he is and what it is he is promoting. Copies or examples will, naturally, be included with this letter, where appropriate.]

. . . Could you look over this —— and, if favourably impressed, provide us with a one- or two-line endorsement note? The endorsement will be used in direct mail and display advertisements. If you so express the wish, we can send you a copy of anything using your name before it is actually published.

If you do decide to provide us with an endorsement, please spell out how you want your identification line to read, including your current title, latest book published, and so on.

With best wishes,

Yours sincerely,

Curiously enough, people do respond and they hand over their golden promotional line like this:

SPECIMEN LETTER 34: TESTIMONIAL/ENDORSEMENT

Dear Mr . . .

I'd be happy to give an endorsement for the ———. What about the following:

> 'Totally helpful, totally witty, the ——— will help you with your ——— needs. Every ——— deserves access to this service which provides accuracy and preserves good humour.'

> Landon Dance,
> Professor of Communications, University of ———

I hope that's of some help.

Yours sincerely,

But what if you do not wish to give an endorsement? For years I have been intrigued by those little puffs you find on the covers of novels, especially American ones, in which a Well-Known Person writes something flattering about the contents – 'This is the book that I would like to have written' – Jeffrey Archer; 'Another little gem' – Frank Muir.

Although these sound like extracts from reviews, they are no more than endorsements solicited by the publishers through the method of sending an advance copy to the Well-Known Person who, so they hope, will look upon the work favourably and make appropriately supportive noises. If he or she does not, then presumably whatever he or she comes up with will not find its way on to the book's dust jacket or into blurbs and advertisements for the book. But it is a questionable process and, surely, of *un*-measurable value in attracting purchasers. I suspect that most book-buyers on seeing Frederick Forsyth endorsing the latest Jilly Cooper novel, or whatever the combination is, will merely assume that they are all part of the same mutual promotion network and pay no attention.

So what do Well-Known Persons do when asked to supply a testimonial – particularly if the author is known personally to them?·Well, they could, kindly and generously, provide exactly what is needed. Or, if they do not feel so inclined, they could try writing something equivocal along the lines of Disraeli's 'I shall lose no time in reading it'. They won't be able to get away with Groucho Marx's blurb for an S.J. Perelman book:

'From the moment I picked up your book until I laid it down, I was convulsed with laughter. Some day I intend reading it.' That has been used before. They could say, 'Now this is what I call a book!' or 'I have never read a book like this before!' or 'I shall always treasure this book'.

It could be, of course, that you are not opposed to the principle of providing endorsements but don't like the particular product or service you have been asked to recommend. I was once asked to provide an endorsement for a comic novel which I found to be completely unreadable, but I did not wish to disappoint the publisher by refusing. So I came up with something unusable like, 'Reminds me of Hieronymous Bosch at his peak . . .'

But the best way out, on balance, is politely to decline the invitation, saying you have 'always made it a rule not to' and that this 'unfortunately makes it impossible to recommend' things that you do like.

Clearly this is not a dilemma that every one of us will face, but it provides an interesting angle on the question of the solicited compliment which the average person is more likely to encounter when asked to give references (as above).

Opened in error

It is customary practice within the business environment to make a written note of apology if you have mistakenly opened an envelope intended for another person. It is quite an easy mistake to perform. Putting 'Opened in error' with your initials or signature (however illegible) is curiously reassuring to the person whose envelope has been violated. Otherwise it is a bit like having had a burglar rummaging in your desk.

Copy catalogue

It is good business practice to make it clear whenever a copy of a letter has been sent to a third party. Simply putting 'Copies to Angela Browne, Dick White . . . [or 'A.B., R.W.', or their job titles]' or 'c.c. Angela Browne, Dick White . . .' is all that is necessary.

Letters of agreement

An important use for letters in business is to set down the terms of an agreement between two parties in a specific way. As is generally known, a 'verbal contract' is perfectly good in law, but it is understandable that the parties to a more complicated agreement will wish, and will need, to have something more tangible to hold on to and refer to. Besides, a 'letter of agreement' is a good deal friendlier than your average contract as drawn up by a lawyer. It can also be couched in more human language, though just as much care needs to be taken in the wording of the sentences. A letter of agreement has just as much validity as a formal legal contract but could be subjected to attack by lawyers who may feel they have been done out of a fee . . .

The form is for one of the parties to an agreement to draw up a letter and send it to the other(s) for approval. If this is arrived at, then the first party sends two copies of the finished agreement to the second party/ parties (having already signed and dated both of the copies). The second party/parties signs both copies, returns one and keeps the other for his or her records.

SPECIMEN LETTER 35: LETTER OF AGREEMENT (i)

[Headed notepaper, if appropriate; address of originator]
[Address of co-signatory]   29 April 199–

Dear Bob,

I am writing to set out terms of an agreement between us for you to
. . . Until this agreement is terminated by either one of us, in
consultation with the other, I undertake not to permit any other
person to. . . . You are also entitled to seek . . . anywhere in the
world except for the United Kingdom.

Each quarter year, I undertake to supply on computer disk
sufficient data to enable you to produce. . . . For your part, you
undertake to use your best efforts to promote and sell . . .in the
territories mentioned.

It is understood between us that after your necessary expenses
have been deducted from revenue, the balance of any profit will be
divided equally between us. Every six months you will pay to me my
share by cheque . . . together with a reasonably detailed account of
the income and expenditure. These statements and payments
should be drawn up to the 31st December and the 30th June
each year. I should not be required to contribute additionally to any
of your start-up costs, merely to provide the matter already mentioned.

In due course I will register the name of the product as a trade mark in the. . . . I also undertake to do such promotional work as I am able to do, as we both agree is necessary.

Should it prove impossible for either one of us to continue to fulfil his part in this agreement, we will work together to find suitable replacements or seek to recompense customers for any unused portions of their payments. In any event, you would not be entitled to sell the product without my permission. Our respective heirs, executors and administrators should respect the intentions of this agreement, in the event of our deaths. I look forward very much to working with you on this project and thank you for suggesting it.

Yours sincerely,

SIGNED S.T.U.   AGREED & SIGNED P.Q.R.
DATE   DATE

It is also quite in order for a contract of employment to be drawn up in the form of a simple exchange of letters.

SPECIMEN LETTER 36: LETTER OF AGREEMENT (ii)

MOUSE ELECTRONICS
Deansgate House, Oxford Street, Manchester M3 2XP
Tel. 061-X84-6994

Thomas Sharp
38, Twistleton Lane
Tarporley
Cheshire
CH1 1UE   2 September 199–

Dear Mr Sharp,

I am pleased to offer you, on behalf of Mouse Electronics, an appointment as a Mouse Trainee, on the following terms. This offer is subject to the receipt of references satisfactory to us.

1. Your engagement will cover the period 3 October 199- to 3 March 199-.

2. You will receive from us remuneration at the rate of £300 per week payable weekly.

3. Notwithstanding the fixed term of this agreement, your engagement will be subject to four weeks' notice on either side.

4. Should you complete the training course to our satisfaction and should we then propose offering you employment with this Company in another capacity, we undertake to notify you in writing by 6 February 199- of the terms and conditions on which our offer would be based.

5. You will be based in Manchester but on occasion may be required to work elsewhere.

6. We will reimburse you reasonable and necessary out-of-pocket expenses incurred by you in the course of your duties.

7. You are not eligible for membership of the Company's Life Assurance and Pension Scheme.

8. You will not at any time either during or after the termination of this Agreement, disclose to any person whatsoever any information relating to the Company, its products, or any trade secrets of which you become possessed whilst employed under this Agreement to any person not authorized to receive the same.

Would you please confirm your acceptance of this by signing and returning the enclosed copy of this letter to the Personnel Department.

Yours sincerely,

R.D. Probert
Personnel Manager

RDP/MB

This strikes me as being a no-nonsense way of setting out essential points. If the letter is not exactly full of human warmth – and how could it be? – it largely avoids legalisms, notwithstanding the use of 'notwithstanding'. 'Whatever' would have done just as well as 'whatsoever'.

Your cheque is in the post

The successful pursuit of debts by letter is a forlorn matter. Nothing can compare with the physical presence of the debtee when reminding the debtor of his or her obligations. However, it is more than likely that initial indications and reminders of overdue payments will be sent through the post.

These days, the fact that a debt has been or is being incurred tends to be signalled by computer and a brusque letter of demand is despatched automatically. This is regrettable. No one likes to receive demands coated in red ink, coupled with dire threats of disconnection, summons, or eternal damnation. Clearly the person or organization pursuing the debt needs to decide which is worse – being too soft, in case a mistake has been made, there is reasonable doubt, etc., or using language which may offend the customer or client.

In business, as in private life, it is just as effective, however, to adopt a tone of feigned puzzlement when pursuing debts. Of course, it is an 'oversight', the delay is not 'intentional', and you are sure that the customer will take immediate steps to 'remedy the situation' or get in touch with you 'if there has been a mistake on our part'. This diplomatic approach can soon be dropped if it is seen to be not working.

SPECIMEN LETTER 37: DEMAND NOTE

[Headed notepaper – which must carry a contact phone number]

[Address of debtor]   [Date]

Dear Mr Abercrombie,

Our records show that the sum of £— is owing and overdue from you as part of your agreement with us, number A20045637Y.

We must remind you that, under your agreement with us, payments are due to reach us on the first day of each month. The agreement also provides for repossession of the goods if you fall behind with your payments.

I am sure there is a good explanation for your late payment on this occasion. If you have paid any moneys in within the last seven days, please ignore this letter. You will appreciate that it takes several working days for payments to be processed by the clearing banks.

If you wish to speak to me about this matter, please ring the number shown at the top of this letter.

Yours sincerely,

Maureen Bishop
Customer Services Assistant

MB/1

The important thing is for you, as the debtee, not to lose your rag and risk alienating valued and innocent customers. Even if you feel you are having to feign understanding of the debtor's probable plight, do so. It is just possible that there has been some terrible mistake, you have in fact been paid the money and the computer has erred, and there is no point in playing the heavy when you are going to have to grovel along with apologies if a mistake becomes apparent.

A resignation matter

As stated in Chapter 9, page 157, there is no place in business or professional resignation letters for the settling of scores or for attempting to position your stake in the moral high ground. The tone of resignation letters should always be courteous and factual. Resignation letters should never be written in the white heat of controversy or in order to play to a wider audience. All they require is the calm recital of a fact and an intention. Even if the calmness is feigned it is still important not to commit to paper any views that you may subsequently come to regret.

SPECIMEN LETTER 38: RESIGNATION LETTER

24, Harbord Road
London
PE1 1XP
Tel. 08-X32 4964

Roderick Chapman
Minimum Video
Pasta House
Southern Business Park
Greenwich
LONDON
PP1 8SS

12 June 199–

Dear Mr Chapman,

When we talked earlier today, I hope I made it plain to you that I was unhappy with the way Minimum Video was being run and, especially, with my part in the newly enlarged organization.

I think it would be best if I pursued my interests elsewhere and I am now writing formally to give you four weeks' notice of the termination of my contract. I should be grateful if you could acknowledge this letter.

Thank you for allowing me to work with the company for the past five years. Apart from our recent difficulties, I have much enjoyed the experience and hope that I have contributed to its lasting growth.

With best wishes,

Yours sincerely,

Humphrey Evans

SPECIMEN LETTER 39: ACCEPTANCE OF RESIGNATION

Minimum Video Pasta House Southern Business Park
Greenwich LONDON PP1 8SS Tel. 081-5X5 8000

Humphrey Evans
24, Harbord Road
London
PE1 1XP

14 June 199-

Dear Mr Evans,

Thank you for your letter of 12 June indicating that you were
resigning from your contract with our company. While technically
you owe us four weeks' notice in writing, it is unlikely that we would
wish to hold you to this. Aidan Hand of Personnel will be in touch
with you very soon to discuss this matter.

I should like to thank you for your five years of service to the
company and wish you every success in your future activities.

Yours sincerely,

Roderick Chapman

Rather clipped, but not giving anything away. The tone is courteous and
avoids giving the resigner the slightest cause for a tantrum (or legal
action). Indeed, it may almost make him feel rather regretful about
having resigned at all – and this is no doubt partly the intention.

Signing off

It is surprising how many business letters are unintentionally not signed
(i.e. left blank) by the sender. Presumably, the letter has been prepared
from dictation by a secretary and put straight into its envelope. This, to

my mind, is as brusque – if not more so – than using the 'p.p.' technique. It removes any trace of humanity and personality from the letter if a letter is not signed by the person who is sending it.

Long ago, when I first committed this sin – or rather simply forgot to sign a typed letter – I received a gentle rap on the knuckles from the person I sent it to. 'I note that your letter was unsigned. Don't worry, I often do it myself.' Ouch – and quite right, too.

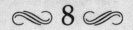

8

DEAR MANAGER

This chapter deals with business and professional correspondence *on the outside* – when customer or client is trying to get some response from, or when customer or client has to respond to letters from, commercial organizations or officialdom.

A basic example of the letter addressed to a business organization *from the outside* is that to your bank manager containing instructions.

 SPECIMEN LETTER 40: INSTRUCTIONS TO BANK
MANAGER

29, Cedarville Road
Loughburdell
Snoddwell
Bankshire
ZY3 8PP

The Manager
Westnat Bank PLC
59, The High Street
CLEARING
Bankshire
ZZ1 6HH   1 January 199-

Dear Manager,

Moneygrabber Account 113294055

I should like to give 90 days' notice for the withdrawal of £2,500 from the above account. Please credit this sum to my Feeble Interest Cheque Account 555594032 when appropriate.

> Meanwhile, I should like to have some acknowledgement that you
> have received this instruction.
>
> Yours sincerely

Bald and to the point, one hopes. Note the 'Dear Manager' – yet again I have to emphasize that this is the simplest way out of the 'Dear Sir or Madam' dilemma and allows you to sign 'Yours sincerely' with perfect correctness. The giving of account numbers shows the bank what it needs to know and that you are speaking its language. The 'Meanwhile . . .' sentence is vital. Without receiving an acknowledgement you have no idea whether your letter has reached its target and been acted upon. I have known such instructions disappear into a deep void – and been charged for the resulting overdrafts – so it is worth being very heavy on this matter. A telephone call (provided you make a note of when and from whom it came) will give you at least a leg to stand on.

As it happens, acknowledgement of this instruction was received by return of post, in these terms: 'Dear Mr ——, We write to confirm the receipt of your letter dated . . . giving 90 Days' Notice for the withdrawal of £2,500 from your Moneygrabber account . . . The instructions to transfer the above amount to your Feeble Interest Cheque Account will be processed on 1 April. Yours sincerely . . . Customer Services Manager.' Well done!

F.A.O.

Even these days, when the cult of personality is rife in big business, it is still possible for confusion to reign as to who exactly you are dealing with when you write to a company or organization. Should you address your letter to the company as a whole or to an individual (if you can identify the responsible one)?

No one likes to send off a letter to a heap of bricks and mortar or to a vague spiritual concept. Letters are best addressed to people, so it makes sense to take some trouble in finding out who in a large organization you should aim to correspond with. Even if this requires a preliminary phone call to the switchboard: 'Can you tell me the name of your Customer Services Manager/Managing Director/Chairman . . . and how are you spelling that? . . . and he's at the Tower Street address, right?'

Some organizations encourage corporate anonymity, however. They may even refuse to disclose names over the telephone. They may send you prepaid envelopes which bear only the name of the company. Are you sure that it is safe to allow the post-room of some vast conglomerate to direct your humble missive to the right employee?

Better – and quicker, probably – to do your own targeting. Put 'F.A.O. [For the Attention Of] Derek Roberts' on the front or back of the envelope.

The debtor's whine

If you get into debt or fall behind with agreed payments, it is probable that you will initially be alerted to your shortcomings by a letter from the person or organization to whom you owe the money. It is an unfortunate (and not entirely necessary) fact that such demand notes are usually insensitive. The use of verbal threats is thought likely, and quite wrongly, to produce a rapid resolution of this little crisis. Would that companies did not reach for the red ink so readily (as discussed in Chapter 7, page 123).

If you are in debt, it behoves you to acknowledge the fact both to yourself and to your creditor. Ignoring the debt will not make it go away. As many large organizations, the Inland Revenue, banks, and so on have discovered, it pays to listen to what their debtors have to say and to start a dialogue. That way, a more realistic schedule of repayments may be arranged. Or, at least, your creditor will be given some insight into the human dimensions and practicalities of the problem. It is a fact that many creditors will gladly settle for less than the whole sum owed if they are able to establish some form of direct dialogue with the debtor and if, in this way, they are made to feel hopeful that the rest of the sum will eventually be paid one day.

SPECIMEN LETTER 41: DEBTOR TO CREDITOR

The Cringe
29, Mincing Lane
Hardup
Bankruptshire
HA18 7UY

The Credit Manager
Pasta House
Southern Business Park
LONDON
PP1 8SS   1 February 199–

Dear Credit Manager,

Thank you for your letter of 12 March regarding the overdue payments on my ——.

Unfortunately, I have recently made redundant at work – a fact which you are most probably not aware of – and I am experiencing difficulty in raising funds while I am in the process of signing on for unemployment benefit.

I fully recognize my obligation to keep my payments up but I hope you will understand the difficult situation I am facing. I should very much appreciate it if I could talk to one of your staff about what might be done in this situation and to find out what the alternatives are.

I look forward to hearing from you.

Yours sincerely

This knocks the ball back into the Credit Manager's court, however temporarily. Above all, it proves that the writer is not trying to be elusive. He provides information – which, it is true, he should probably already have given to the Manager – and shows a willingness to sort out the problem. He indicates that he is not intending to avoid the debt and shows an eagerness to find a way of resolving the matter.

When words fail

It is when people who are not used to writing find themselves *having* to put words on paper that some very odd things occur. Nowhere is this more the case than in the field of insurance claims, particularly where car drivers attempt to summarize details of accidents involving them – in the least possible number of words. Their shortcomings have become the stuff of comedians' patter, but these examples (genuine, I am assured, and sent to an insurance company's offices in Hereford) are worth quoting if only to underline how important it is to take a little trouble to check whatever you have written before posting it off *whatever the subject of your letter*. Try to ensure that your words express what you want them to say and that they cannot also be misinterpreted in other ways. If the letters from which these extracts are taken had been drafted first, surely most of these clangers (however delicious) would have been removed.

- The telephone pole was approaching, I was attempting to swerve out of the way when I struck the front end.
- An invisible car came from nowhere, struck my car and vanished.
- I collided with a stationary truck coming the other way.
- Coming home I drove into the wrong house and collided with a tree I don't have.
- The other car collided with mine without giving warning of its intention.
- I thought my window was down, but I found out it was up when I put my head through it.
- A truck backed through my windshield into my wife's face.
- The guy was all over the road. I had to swerve a number of times before I hit him.
- I pulled away from the side of the road, glanced at my mother-in-law and headed over the embankment.
- In an attempt to kill a fly, I drove into a telegraph pole.
- I had been shopping for plants all day and was on my way home. As I reached an intersection a hedge sprung up, obscuring my vision, and I did not see the other car.
- I had been driving for forty years when I fell asleep at the wheel and had an accident.
- I was on my way to the doctor's with rear end trouble when my universal joint gave way, causing me to have an accident.
- As I approached the intersection, a sign suddenly appeared in a place where no stop sign had ever appeared before. I was unable to stop in time to avoid the accident.
- To avoid hitting the bumper in front, I struck the pedestrian.
- My car was legally parked as it backed into the other vehicle.
- I told the police that I was not injured, but on removing my hat, found that I had a fractured skull.
- I was sure the old fellow would never make it to the other side of the road when I struck him.
- The pedestrian had no idea which way to run, so I ran over him.
- I saw a slow-moving, sad-faced old gentleman as he bounced off the roof of my car.
- The indirect cause of the accident was a little guy in a small car with a big mouth.
- I was thrown from my car as it left the road. I was later found in a ditch by some stray cows.

Dear Teacher

I am putting this immediately after the insurance claims for a very good reason. Letters from parents to school teachers informing them of domestic problems directly concerning their pupils also give rise to some spectacular errors. Why is it that they do? Presumably because parents have to dash them off before they have woken up properly. All they need to do is write this:

 SPECIMEN LETTER 42: LETTER TO TEACHER

56, School Road
Winstanley
Derbyshire
DS2 9UH

(No telephone)

4 February, 199-

Dear Miss Cartwright,

I am afraid Colin is unable to attend school today as he has been taken ill with the 'flu.

The doctor is coming to see him later today. I would expect Colin to be back at school by Thursday at the latest.

With best wishes,

Yours sincerely,

[+ Legible signature + any additional identification to enable the teacher to know who is being talked about. The parentage and guardianship of children these days is so complicated that it should be made clear exactly which pupil is being talked about, using the name that the child has been registered under. It is helpful if the signatory of the letter makes it clear who he or she is: parent, step parent, guardian or whatever.]

The consequences of not being straightforward and sensibly factual in 'parental' notes are terrible to relate. From teachers' archives come these 'parental' blunders:

Dear Miss,

Please excuse Mary from having a shower, being how she is. Being how you are yourself sometimes, you will understand how she is.

Dear Miss,

Our Johnnie came home with a big hole in his trousers, will you please look into it?

Dear Miss,

Please excuse Sandra being late. She was waiting for the bus at twenty to nine but came back to use the toilet and missed it.

Dear Miss,

Sorry Jim is late but me and my husband rather overdone it this morning.

Dear Miss,

I have not sent Johnny to school this morning because he hasn't been. I have given him something to make him go, and when he's been he'll come.

Curriculum vitae

There are few aspects of letter writing more important than when a letter is required to get you a job – so much so that specific tuition can be provided to help people with written job applications. It is equally possible to have your job application written for you, for a fee.

Why this should be necessary is because – according to people who have to process job applications – many, possibly most, forms of writing submitted to them show signs of poor presentation and thought, if not of misspelling and illiteracy. It is an obvious point, but one too often ignored, that no one is going to give you a job if you can't ask for one properly.

That is the bottom line, as they say. But a job letter requires more than a basic proficiency. It needs to stand out from the hundreds of other letters that the potential employer has to sift through, not just by the way it looks but in terms of its content.

If your calligraphy is astonishing, you might achieve this stand-out effect by writing your letter by hand, but for most of us this would not apply. So the letter *must* be typed, even if you don't know how to type. Find a way. And it must be typed as well as the letter you will eventually receive telling you that you have got the job.

Having said that, giving a smooth professional look to your letter may only mean that you haven't produced a messy, smudged, amateurish application. Your letter will only look smooth and professional . . . like all the other smooth and professional ones. Accordingly, the *content* of the letter must be distinctive and the style individual.

Achieving this is difficult. It is the convention nowadays to separate the details of your education, experience and qualifications from your covering letter, in other words to put the C.V./*curriculum vitae*/'course of life' on a separate sheet of paper. You could be different and somehow weave this information into your main letter but it so much the custom to have the facts of your career listed separately that this might count against you. Put the detail separately.

Still, this only increases the demand on you to make the covering letter attention-grabbing, fresh and original. If you are not used to selling yourself in words, the obvious way of achieving this is to draft, draft and re-draft what you are going to send off. In that way, you will be able to winkle out the clichés, exhume the dullness, or put a damper on too much cockiness.

Incidentally, if you are writing to a large number of potential employers at the same time you will almost certainly end up writing much the same letter to each. However, do not consider for a moment *duplicating* your basic letter (on any sort of copying machine) and filling in the name and address by hand. Any potential employer will notice that you have taken a short cut and can't be bothered to individualize your letter. In fact, duplicated letters of almost any kind are to be avoided wherever possible.

SPECIMEN LETTER 43: APPLYING FOR A SPECIFIC JOB

Brian Kaye
The Personnel Director
Major Engineering PLC
The Works
BIRMINGHAM XX1 2YY   12 September 199–

Dear Mr Kaye,

I was most interested to see your advertisement in today's *Guardian* for Project Managers (Ref. 234) as this is precisely the work I am currently seeking and for which I believe I have the relevant qualifications.

As you will see from the attached C.V., since leaving university with a degree in Civil Engineering, I have gradually moved towards involvement in project management. I have also had specific training under the auspices of the Institute of Project Management and am working towards a qualification.

I would be more than happy to attend for an interview if you feel that my C.V. merits it.

With best wishes,

Yours sincerely,

Enc. CV

Not poetry, but it is short and to the point, it only covers one side of a piece of notepaper, and it is not bumptious.

SPECIMEN LETTER 44: INQUIRING ABOUT GENERAL WORK OPPORTUNITIES

402, Enterprise Way, Brunelville, Birmingham B62 3RQ
Tel. (home) 0X1-353-5555 (work) 0327-X998450

The Personnel Director
Megalopolis PLC
The Ball-Park
LONDON
PP1 1QQ   30 December 199–

Dear Personnel Director,

As you will see from my enclosed C.V., I have experience of several
jobs in the sales and marketing field. I am now actively seeking to
widen my experience and am looking for openings in larger companies than I have worked for till now.

I am therefore writing to see whether there are – or are likely to be –
any openings at Megalopolis, which is a company I have long felt I
should like to work for. It would be of the greatest assistance to me
if you could look at my C.V. and draw my availability to the attention
of anyone in Megalopolis who might be interested.

If it would be of any use, please do not hesitate to call me at my
work number. I should, of course, be very glad to let you have any
further details you require or to attend for an interview.

With best wishes,

Yours sincerely,

Enc. C.V.

Enquiries and complaints

For most people, writing to a company or organization will be in
connection with fiddly administrative matters – enquiring about goods
not received, querying bills, complaining about service or lack of, and so
on. It is a burden for the private individual to have to type such letters
rather than dash them off by hand, but it gives a touch more authority to
the letter if it is typed, as well as being easier for the receiver to deal
with.

As in all business correspondence, the greater degree of formality required as compared with personal letter writing should not be mistaken for pomposity and verbosity. The formality resides in the detail and nature of information supplied in an 'official communication' rather than in the tone of voice, which can nevertheless remain quite personal. Indeed, the more personality you allow to shine through, the more likely you are to make human contact with the otherwise anonymous organization you may be dealing with.

It may be argued that this type of communication is better done by telephone. Against that you may have to set (1) the difficulty of identifying who precisely within a large organization you should speak to, (2) the cost in money and personal wear and tear of having to hang on to a telephone while you are shunted around a large organization, and (3) the possible difficulty in having your problem dealt with adequately when all your details are not down on paper in front of the person who ends up dealing with the problem.

A little bit of both may be in order – by which I mean, send a letter first, followed by a phone call. The phone call should either be soon, to impress upon the company that you mean business even if they don't, or after a while, when you feel that your letter is clearly not being attended to.

SPECIMEN LETTER 45: ENQUIRING ABOUT GOODS NOT RECEIVED

89, Woodstock Avenue
Worple Heath
Surrey
SU8 5XT

Tel. 01X6-675849

The Manager
Bedding Department
Slumbering & Snoring Ltd
39, Wooden Stairs
BEDFORD
Bedfordshire
ZZ1 1ZZ   4 October 199–

Dear Manager,

Order no. 706040

My order for a Grosvenor Put-U-Up bed was placed on 13 July and I was told that delivery would probably take from four to six weeks. Now that nearly three months have passed, I am beginning to wonder if there has been some problem.

I should be grateful if you would either phone or write to me confirming that matters are proceeding as planned.

Looking forward to hearing from you.

Yours sincerely

Enclosing a photocopy of the original order might astound the shop at how organized you are, as well as making it easier for them to pinpoint the order, thus facilitating a reply.

SPECIMEN LETTER 46: COMPLAINING OF FAULTS IN
GOODS OBTAINED BY MAIL ORDER

89, Woodstock Avenue
Worple Heath
Surrey
SU8 5XT

Tel. 01X6-675849

Good Workmanship Cooperative
Unit 200,The Business Park
MILTON KEYNES
RR1 2SS 1 June 199-

Dear Good Workmanship Cooperative,

Sunday Telegraph Special Offer Work Tidy
Order no. 3950

After having waited 46 days rather than the 28 you advertised for the delivery of my work tidy, I was immensely disappointed on taking the item out of its packing when it did arrive to discover that the woodwork had been chipped in two places. This was only apparent after the item was unpacked and after I had signed receipt of delivery. It was obviously impractical for me to unpack and examine the goods while the delivery driver was waiting at my door.

I am sure that this damage must have occurred in the post after the goods left your factory but I wonder if the packing was sufficient to protect the goods? It would obviously be very inconvenient and difficult for me to have to arrange the return of such a large item to your factory, so I would be obliged if you would let me have your views on the matter as soon as possible.

Yours sincerely,

Again, a photocopy of the delivery note would help support this complaint – not the actual delivery note, as you may need that.

This letter is about nine parts bluff. Its chief aim is to signal to the manufacturer – without overt threatening – that your complaint is serious and that, if they ignore it, you won't let up until they make amends. Note that the writer does not threaten at this stage to 'take the matter further' or to bring in the newspaper or any of the mail order protection schemes. The writer simply lobs the problem back at the manufacturer (possibly not knowing what form of compensation can or should be forthcoming).

The writer knows he is on shaky ground – the manufacturer could cite any number of get-out clauses – but he hints that he is aware of the difficulties both sides face in resolving the matter.

In fact, when I had to write a similar letter to a similar outfit on one occasion I quickly received some of my money back. Probably this was not really sufficient to compensate me for the damaged goods or for my trouble in writing the letter. As it happens, I was able to make good the damage myself, but I was spared the bother of parcelling the goods up and sending them back. I subsequently learned that two weeks after I received my compensation cheque, the firm went bust.

SPECIMEN LETTER 47: QUERYING A REQUEST FOR PAYMENT

[Address/Telephone number]

[Date]

Janet Aston
Photocopiers Limited
Greene Science Park
NOTTINGHAM
NN1 1NN

Dear Janet Aston,

Machine number: 29220500008

Thank you for your two notes about the enclosed invoice no. 464426. I now understand that this relates to my new photo-copier. However, I am unable to pay you for two reasons:

1) The invoice is made out to a company which is no longer in existence. The new contract is in my personal name. (It might be a good idea to give me a new account number, to save any further confusion.)

2) As I have attempted to explain to your London Sales Office (which arranged the new contract), the Service Maintenance Agreement I was encouraged to sign is in fact *blank* on the question of the minimum number of copies chargeable. Hence my surprise at being billed for a minimum of 5,000 copies quarterly, which is far in excess of my normal usage.

Clearly, something has gone wrong somewhere along the line and I notice that your Code of Conduct provides for reassessing such matters in the light of a customer's actual needs.

It would obviously be helpful if somebody in your company could take the intiative in sorting this out, as clearly I am not in a position to understand your way of doing things.

Yours sincerely,

Copy to: London Sales Office

When I had to send a similar letter to the 'credit control contact' of a company, it did not produce a very speedy or satisfactory result, though the red ink evaporated from the 'Final demand' notes and was replaced by a symbol showing that the payments in question were 'in dispute'. The letter above is, I hope, patient and firm, not angry. If there is a slightly pained, put-upon air to the last paragraph, it nevertheless declares a very real problem. How is the customer, on the outside, supposed to know – and find out – how things are meant to happen on the inside?

SPECIMEN LETTER 48: COMPLAINING OF POOR
SERVICE

Cottage Industry Ltd
The Barn, Sunrise Valley, Carshalton, Surrey, KT3 4RR
Tel. 034X-456789 Fax. 034X-111222

Luigi Jones
Chairman, Spaghetti
  Computers PLC
Elephant House
Fulham Broadway
London
SW6 7FF   8 February 199–

Dear Mr Jones,

The slogan which your advertising agency has devised for you is 'You're never up a gum tree with Spaghetti Computers'. How is it then that I have been unable to make use of my Pasta 4/33 – which is vital to me in the running of my business – since a week last Thursday?

Despite repeated calls to the service centre for this area, it was not until five days had elapsed that a service engineer arrived to look at the machine. It then had to be taken away to be examined on the bench. At no time was any offer made of a temporary replacement machine.

It seems to me that in your advertising and sales you persuade customers like myself to put extreme reliance on your machines but then, when there is some problem with service personnel, you abandon customers to their fates.

Nothing that you can do could compensate me for the frustration and annoyance I have been caused or for the harm that has been done to my business. But I thought you should be aware of what is going on at the sharp end of your company's affairs – where your staff actually come into contact with customers.

Yours sincerely,

Adrian Hack
Managing Director

As the writer of this letter acknowledges, nothing could really make up for the trouble he has had. So his letter to the Chairman (whose name he had to find out by ringing up the company) is chiefly to do with letting off steam. It is possible, indeed, that the last paragraph is a veiled request for some form of compensation. If so, Adrian Hack knows that he is not going to get it. But he is doing something useful by writing in this manner to the Chairman.

It is just possible that the letter will actually pass before the eyes of the Chairman and won't get fished out and sat upon by some minion. If it does pass before the Chairman's eyes, it could conceivably be a revelation to him as to what is actually going on at the 'sharp end' of the company. It is possible, too, that simply by writing the letter, this 'dissatisfied customer' will begin to recover from his ordeal, and that should be enough.

On the other hand, whether the Chairman will – or could – be seriously challenged or forever altered in his ways by such a letter has to remain in doubt. For the ideal response from a Chairman to this kind of complaint see Chapter 7, specimen letter 29.

SPECIMEN LETTER 49: TO BANK MANAGER QUERYING
CHARGES

[Address/Telephone numbers]

[Date]

The Manager
Westnat Bank PLC
59, The High Street
CLEARING
Bankshire
ZZ1 6HH

Dear Manager,

Current Account no. 987654321

I was surprised to see from my latest statement received today that a sum of £250 has been deducted from my account as 'Charges'. As the account has not gone into the red and I am unaware of any other services supplied to me, I should be very grateful if you could explain this significant charge to me as soon as you can.

As ever, it would be courteous if your bank could give its customers a detailed account of what charges are being made for, without those customers having to ask for it.

Yours sincerely,

I wonder how many letters like this have to be written each month? Given that banks do actually make mistakes and given that they are surprisingly ready to 'try it on' when it comes to charges, customers should always be quick to write back and seek clarification. Given that banks are among the few institutions which are in a position to seize your money without asking you, or telling you in advance, the second paragraph seems more than justified. Harping on it at every opportunity may not do you any good but at least it makes you feel better.

Hotel booking

The elaborate procedure of yesteryear when a hotel reservation made by phone had to be confirmed by letter and then acknowledged by the hotel has now been largely rendered obsolete by the fax machine and the credit card. Giving details of your credit card at the time of booking means that the hotel will keep your room, even should you be delayed beyond your expected arrival time. Naturally, you may still want to have confirmation in writing, by letter or fax, just to have something to wave at the hotel in case of a mistake.

Giving your credit card number does, of course, mean that if you do not show up at all, you will be charged for one night's accommodation and possibly for more if the hotel is unable to let your room to another guest. Should you be unable to take up a booking because you are stuck on an aeroplane, say, this might be painful. Always try to advise a hotel of any late or non-arrival.

When booking, it is always a good idea to get the hotel to tell you precisely how much you will be charged for the room. They may find this rather tiresome (given all the discounts and special rates they are likely to operate) but you should insist and, especially, enquire as to the availability of corporate rates, special schemes and so on. It is a mistake to think that there is only one price on a hotel room.

SPECIMEN LETTER 50: CONFIRMING A HOTEL
RESERVATION

[Address/Telephone numbers]

[Date]

The Manager
The Abbey Hotel
The Promenade
SOUTHPORT
Lancashire
YY1 3TT

Dear Manager,

This is to confirm my telephone reservation made earlier today of one double-bedded room for three nights. We shall be arriving on Friday 21 May and departing on Monday 24 May. Please note that we may not be arriving until about 10 p.m. I believe you mentioned that a special weekend rate of £75 for bed and breakfast would apply. As agreed, the reservation is being held by you against VISA card no. 11111111111 (expiry 9/96).

With my thanks,

Yours sincerely,

This is spelling everything out in great detail. Getting the number of nights right and the arrival and departure dates is what really matters if the booking has already been discussed over the phone. You should, of course, keep a photocopy of the letter if you want to be armed in any regrettable future arguments. Practice varies a lot these days: some hotels will send you a written acknowledgement, some won't. It is all very unsettling.

Writing abroad

It is easy to make fun of foreigners' attempts to write English. Gerald Hoffnung made famous use of letters supposedly received from Tyrolean landladies describing the delights of their properties – 'There is a French widow in every bedroom (affording delightful prospects . . .)' – but most British people are incapable of writing business or semi-business letters in a foreign language. If they try, who knows what howlers they perpetrate?

However, whether it is a good thing or not, English has become the international language, so it is quite permissible to lean heavily on the indulgence of other language speakers. It is surely better to say what you have to say in English and get it right, rather than bungle an attempt at writing in a foreign language. On the other hand, an attempt to write even part of the letter in your recipient's language will be appreciated.

When writing or faxing to foreign countries where you cannot assume that your English will be understood – say you are trying to make a booking at a small hotel in rural France – then it might be an idea to make use of sample booking letters in the language of the country you are dealing with. These may be obtained from most tourist organizations.

When writing to the United States it is natural to loosen up your English to accord with what your correspondent is used to (though it is quite likely the correspondent, in deference to your Britishness, will go all olde-worlde courtesy on you). While you are well-advised to loosen up, I am not in favour of your loading what you write with all sorts of Americanisms. This might appear patronizing. You might also get them wrong. But, all in all, a certain defiant Britishness will do you no harm at all. There is no need to Americanize your spelling but you might prefer to take care not to use any English idioms or allusions which are likely to be lost on your Americans.

And beware the famous differences between British-English and American-English. If your correspondent tells you that he is 'quite interested' in your proposals, do not take offence. In the US 'quite' means 'very' – so get excited instead.

Generally, when writing a letter in English to someone for whom it is a second language or who does not speak British-English, it is wise to write with conscious clarity – both in words used and in handwriting, too. Even if this is the written equivalent of the attitude, 'No, I don't speak foreign languages – I just speak English loudly and very slowly at 'em', it is only sensible to do so. English is so full of idioms and shortened ways of sayings things that it is of great help to the foreigner if you spell things out a bit. The colloquial can be a chore if you are not used to it:

> Dear Heinrich,
>
> Delighted that you coming over next week. We can certainly put you up if you don't mind a bit of domestic squalor (cat's got the squits again, I'm afraid). Don't be alarmed either if my better half is a bit under the weather. Time of the month, you know.
>
> Any road, I'll pick you up from Victoria and we can have a drop or two of the hard stuff before . . .

I think you should have got the message by now. (On the other hand, if the foreigner is a German, he'll probably be your equal in this sort of thing and cap every sentence with 'Don't you know, old chap, toodle pip' and so on.)

Unsolicited correspondence

Dealing with junk mail and unsolicited mail is almost as dispiriting as receiving it. There can be few opening sentences that make the heart sink more than: 'Dear Cardholder, From time to time we see an idea or service which catches our eye. On your behalf we examine it and consider its appeal. . . . Hence this letter to you.' Your reaction will probably be to throw that kind of missive straight into the bin, and quite right too. Commercial junk mail never has to be answered, of course, but there is a certain type of unsought mail that may detain you for a little longer.

People, however loosely in the public eye, receive requests for help and information, even autographs and photographs, which may cost a good deal in terms of time and money. I have seen certain public figures tip unsolicited correspondence straight into the wastepaper basket, the contents barely read and certainly unanswered. Others painstakingly reply to every letter, either with a view to winning popularity or votes, or because they feel that if someone is sufficiently willing to spend money on a stamp and an envelope (even to be rude) then they deserve a reply. But almost anyone may at some time get letters which they may dither over dealing with.

So when does unsolicited correspondence have to be answered? The answer must be, only when you feel like it and *if* you feel like it.

Some requests – to read attempts at fiction or to help someone with their charitable works – can be extremely tedious. If no postage is enclosed for the return of the manuscript, it deserves not to be returned. You can hold on to it, if you have the storage space, in the hope that one day the postage will turn up. Or you can send the stuff back with no postage on, and let the person who has bothered you pick up the bill.

Veterans of this kind of harassment by mail often devise all-purpose printed cards which they can send off with the minimum of thought:

> Thank you for your inquiry but XXXX regrets that it is impossible for him/her to: read manuscripts/judge literary contests/answer questionnaires/donate copies of his/her books to libraries/give advice on how to start a literary career/etc.

Among public figures who have been reduced to this, I am aware of authors like Edmund Wilson, A.J.P. Taylor and George Bernard Shaw. According to Michael Holroyd's biography of Shaw (Vol.2, 1989), the busy author devised a whole set of standard postcard replies. Some of these outlined his stance on issues like capital punishment and temperance, but most were used to say 'no' to requests: 'They spelled out his reasons for being unable to read and report on unpublished manuscripts . . . inscribe books that were not his personal gifts, or comply with requests from strangers for his autograph (with or without a photograph) . . . respond to appeals . . . open bazaars, give lectures, eat or speak at public dinners . . . read or write letters.'

Often enough Shaw then proceeded to embroider these printed cards with handwritten messages. He would even sign his refusals to give autographs.

Edmund Wilson, the American author, had a similar all-purpose effusion: 'Edmund Wilson regrets that it is impossible for him to: . . . answer questionnaires . . . allow his name to be used on letterheads . . . supply personal information about himself . . . supply opinion on literary or other subjects' . . . and so on.

I have to say that, though these distinguished men may have been driven to it, this approach seems a little less than gracious. A scribbled note on a compliments slip – even one not bearing the sender's address and telephone number, to discourage further correspondence – would probably be just as effective, especially if it was a secretary who was doing the scribbling.

The only correct response to *mad* correspondents was formulated a number of years ago by H.L. Mencken, when editor of *American Mercury*. Senders of unsolicited manuscripts were advised:

> Mr Mencken has just entered a Trappist monastery in Kentucky and left strict instructions that no mail was to be forwarded. The enclosed is returned, therefore, for your archives.

Opinion-sharers were sent a postcard bearing the sympathetic but correspondence-concluding message:

> Dear Reader,
> You may be right.

As to dealing with unsolicited mailing shots, junk mail and the like – even telephone selling – there is a contradiction here. Rather as with men shaving, if they were offered the option of never having to bother with shaving again, they would probably turn it down. So, if we were told that we would never receive any unsolicited brochures and advertisements ever again, we might well feel a little disappointed. After all, it does occasionally bring us something that is useful to know about.

It is possible to have your name and address removed from mailing lists, officially, and sometimes organizations with membership lists, like charities and credit companies, and which sell mailing lists on to advertisers, give you the option to have your name and address withheld. But no one can guarantee that your name and address will be removed from every existing list, everywhere. The Mailing Preference Service, as it is known, can be contacted at:

1, Leeward House
Square Rigger Row
Plantation Wharf
LONDON
SW11 3TX

Fervent anti-junk mail campaigners return the material to sender without using any postage and enclose a duplicated request for their names to be removed from any lists. Or they make use of any prepaid envelopes and cards to convey this message back to the sender. How far this works I am not sure, but, if nothing else, it helps the anti-junk mail campaigners get things off their chests.

When to send an S.A.E.

If you are writing to another person, soliciting information or help, when should you enclose a self-addressed and stamped envelope, and when not? Well, obviously if an s.a.e. was requested, you would, but otherwise I do not think you need automatically send one. If, for example, the person you are writing to is a professional or business person, then he or she may well be able to claim the expense of any such correspondence off tax. They may also view such correspondence as an inevitable part of their work. If you are writing to a private individual, however, it might well be the case – though not necessarily – that sending an s.a.e. would actively encourage, if not ensure, a reply.

Incidentally, it is not correct to write 'J.N. Enquirer, Esq.' on a self-addressed envelope. You may use 'Mr' (or 'Mrs/Miss/Ms' if a woman), even though these titles can normally only be bestowed upon you by another. In this context, however, it is correct to put one of them on your s.a.e. before sending it off, if you wish to. Presumably the logic is that you are doing the addressing on the sender's behalf.

P.S.

And, finally, as a P.S. . . . and last but not least . . . some rather special letters. Possibly these are not the kind that you can be taught. Possibly some are not the kind you should be encouraged to write at all. But here they are nevertheless – a wide variety of them – and necessary to make this survey of letter writing as complete as possible.

Literary letters

It has not been the purpose of this book to encourage you to write letters that will one day be anthologized – but, on the other hand, why not? What could be more wonderful than to write a letter that acquires some measure of immortality through publication?

In the deep 'writing fields' of literature there are some oddities. For example, if you write a letter – any letter – you hold the copyright, but the person you send it to actually *owns* the letter, the piece of paper. Thus the receiver can sell it but may still not be in a position to reproduce it: a nice dispute can be in the making between writer and receiver.

It also appears that whereas copyright protection expires fifty years after the death of an author, the copyright of a letter writer continues, in theory, indefinitely beyond that date. So watch out!

Love letters in the sand

Because we have never been apart from each other for very long – from the day we first met – I find it rather curious to have to admit that my wife and I have never exchanged letters, of any kind, whatsoever. What a dreadful shame! As a result, you are not about to find me providing specimen love letters.

In any case, that would be a complete contradiction in terms. A love letter by its very nature has to be an intensely personal communication from one person to the other. Nevertheless, there have been numerous documented occasions – especially during wartime – of those people who did have a way with the pen (or who were simply more literate) being called upon to write love letters on behalf of others. But no. All I can do is to observe what a love letter should contain, particularly between lovers who are far apart.

The chief topic and, indeed, the whole purpose of the letter is to bridge the gap between the two people, or to express through the written word what it is difficult to put in the spoken word. It is always fitting to emphasize in a love letter the burden that the separation is putting on the writer and to state how the other person is always in the writer's thoughts. If you can do it as well as the poet Rupert Brooke did in a letter from New York to his actress love, Cathleen Nesbitt, in 1913, you will be doing well:

> Oh, it's Saturday evening, and if I were in England I might be lying on the sofa in Kensington, or on the floor in Gray's Inn, and my head in your lap, and your face bent down over mine, and your hands about my head, and my eyes shut, and I only feeling your hands going to and fro in my hair and your kind lips wandering over my face. And I'm here in a dirty room and lonely and tired and ill, and this won't get to you for ten days.
>
> I'm crying. I want you. I don't want to be alone.
>
> Rupert.

The poet and painter Dante Gabriel Rossetti contrived to create a sense of physical togetherness when he wrote to Mrs Jane Morris (a favourite model of his) in 1870:

> Dear Janey, I suppose this has come into my head because I feel so badly the want of speaking to you. No one else seems alive at all to me now, and places that are empty of you are empty of all life. And it is so seldom that the dead hours breathe a little and yield your dear voice to me again. I seem to hear it while I write, and to see your eyes speaking as clearly as your voice; and so I would write to you forever if it were not too bad to keep reminding you of my troubles, who have so many of your own.

The same Sir Richard Steele as quoted in Chapter 5, page 61, managed to convey his state of mind in a vivid way when writing to Mary Scurlock (whom he married a few days after this letter was sent) in 1707:

> Madam – It is the hardest thing in the World to be in Love and yet attend business. As for Me, all who speak to Me find Me out. . . . A Gentlemen ask'd me this morning what news from Lisbon, and I answer'd She's exquisitely handsome. Another desir'd to know when I had been last at Hampton-Court, I reply'd Twill be on Tuesday come se'nnight [Tuesday week]. Prithee Allow Me at least to Kisse Your Hand before that day, that my mind may be in some Composure. Oh Love!

Writers of love letters should say what they have been doing while apart from the loved one – without, of course, appearing to have been enjoying things too much on their own.

As for the type of love letter which is not between established lovers but is intended to bring about such a situation – well, I can but recall a Chinese student who was part of a theatrical group to which I once belonged. He became very smitten with one of the girls among us but instead of chatting her up, face to face, he wrote her letter. Rather sweetly, he enclosed a stamped addressed envelope for her reply.

'*Epistola enim non erubescit*' ('For a letter does not blush'). – Cicero (*d.* 43BC), *Epistles*, Book 5, line 12

'Sir, more than kisses, letters mingle souls;
For, thus friends absent speak.' – John Donne, *Letters to Severall Personages* (Sir Henry Wotton) (before April 1598)

'Love is the life of friendship; letters are
The life of love.' – James Howell (1594?-1666), *Touching the Vertu and the Use of Familiar Letters*

'As keys do open chests,
So letters open breasts.' – ibid.

'Love is the marrow of friendship, and letters are the Elixir of love.' – ibid.

'And oft the pangs of absence to remove
By letters, soft interpreters of love.' – Matthew Prior, 'Henry and Emma' (1709)

'O well's me o' my gay goss-hawk,That he can speak and flee!
He'll carry a letter to my love,
Bring another back to me.' – Ballad, *The Gay Gosshawk* (date unknown)

'You bid me burn your letters. But I must forget you first.' – John Adams
in a letter to Abigail Adams (28 April 1776)

'He thought he saw an Elephant,
That practised on a fife:
He looked again, and found it was
A letter from his wife.
"At length I realize," he said,
"The bitterness of life!"' – Lewis Carroll, *Sylvie and Bruno*, Chap. 5 (1889)

'You don't know a woman until you have had a letter from her.' – Ada
Leverson, *Tenterhooks*, Chap. 7 (1912)

'A love letter sometimes costs more than a three-cent stamp.' – American
proverb

'The only kind of letters a woman likes to receive from a man are those
which should not have been written.' – Anon.

Dear John . . .

A 'Dear John' (sometimes known as a 'dearjohn') is the name given to a
brush-off letter sent from a wife to a husband (originally it was this way
round) breaking off their relationship because she had formed another
one. Any attempt to break the news gently to the recipient was probably
doomed from the start, especially as the original context was of a
woman carrying on with someone at home while the lover was away
fighting in the armed forces.

The term appears to have arisen in the United States during the
Second World War, as this mention from the *Democrat & Chronicle* of
Rochester, New York, dated 17 August 1945, makes clear: ' "Dear John",
the letter began. "I have found someone else whom I think the world of.
I think the only way out is for us to get a divorce," it said. They usually
began like that, those letters that told of infidelity on the part of the
wives of servicemen. . . . The men call them "Dear Johns".'

The term then became applied to a letter from a woman to her fiancé
breaking off their engagement. Now, I would say, the term is used of
any letter breaking off a relationship, and written by a member of either

sex. It is probably the only way to break the news with the least amount of pain. A face-to-face announcement might be unpleasant and might well prove impossible to stick to if the result was an emotional argument.

An element of calculation as well as consideration should therefore enter the writer's mind. What effect will the letter have? When is it likely to be received? Just as the recipient is going off to work? Should it be delivered by hand at a more appropriate time, to cushion the impact?

Then what should the letter contain? The clichés of this sort of thing are to begin by writing, 'Some letters are as hard to write as they are to receive. This is one of them . . .'. 'I've been thinking about our relationship', 'I wonder if you agree with me that when you can't grow, go?' but these may be hard to avoid.

The decision to split up should be stated, though, as positively and irrevocably as it can be. Let the recipient down as gently as you possibly can. Say, if appropriate, that you have enjoyed the time you have spent with the other person and that you will always remember it happily. End with 'I hope we will always be friends', or some such expression, but consider whether you should invite the disappointed person to ring you for a chat, or whether this might only lead to wrangling and that such an invitation might be a mistake. It is unlikely, however, that a harsh and sudden breaking off of relations will ever be greeted with equanimity, so there is much to be said for contriving a letter that really does anticipate the recipient's queries and demands and that succinctly draws a line under what is past. If it is any consolation, writing letters of this kind has never been easy. In this passage from the novel *Tom Brown at Oxford* (1861), Thomas Hughes puts his hero through it:

Tom went to his own rooms, and set to work to write his letter; and certainly found it as difficult and unpleasant a task as he had ever set himself to work upon. Half a dozen times he tore up sheet after sheet of his attempts . . . and then he sat down again, and wrote, and scratched out what he had written, till the other fit came on, and something of the same process had to be gone through again.

[He shows the letter to his friend Hardy] and watched his face while he read:- 'It is best for us both that I should not see you any more, at least at present. I feel that I have done you a great wrong. I dare not say much to you, for fear of making that wrong greater . . . [and so on].'

'What do you think?' You don't think there's anything wrong in it, I hope?'

'No, indeed, my dear fellow. I really think it does you credit. I don't know what else you could have said very well, only – '

'Only what?'

'Couldn't you have made it a little shorter?' . . .

[Tom admits that he has, in fact, already sent the letter and Hardy comments] 'In that case I don't think we need trouble ourselves further with the form of the document.'

'Oh, that's only shirking. How do you know I may not want it for the next occasion?'

'No, no!. . . . A man never ought to have to write such letters twice in his life. If he has, why he may get a good enough precedent for the second out of the "Complete Letter Writer" . . .'

You see, they had books to help with letter writing even in 1861 . . .

Charitable appeals

Responding to a charitable appeal is entirely up to the person who receives it, but if you have received a genuinely personal letter soliciting charity, perhaps from someone known to you, a reply may be called for. Try not to make it pompous – in which category I would put this from an executive (with whom I had worked many years previously) of a company I had approached on behalf of a well-known charity:

Dear Nigel Rees,

Your letter on behalf of the Motor Neurone Disease Association is persuasive and could not fail to evoke a sympathetic response from any humane reader.

I cannot undertake that this company will contribute because we have a policy of supporting charities only within our area and it is always hard to make an exception for any cause, however good. Although my reply must be almost certainly negative, I will make enquiries and if I can see a way of helping, I will do so.

Not surprisingly nothing ever turned up. The explanation was worth having (though made me want to shout back that although the charity was not based in his company's 'area', some people with the disease undoubtedly *did* live there) but, as I say, the pomposity was not.

Of course, it can be irksome to receive endless demands on one's charitable instincts. I suspect that most people either respond to a printed plea or put it in the waste paper basket. A genuinely personal plea does, however, require some form of response. Lord Erskine, the lawyer who was England's Lord Chancellor from 1806 to 1807, was always being asked to subscribe to various causes and developed a standard (albeit handwritten) response. He would write: 'Sir, I feel much honoured by your application to me, and I beg to subscribe . . .' – here the reader would have to turn over the page – '. . . myself your very obedient servant . . .'

Between you, me, and the Post Office

Is there anything to be said about letters to people who are not, for whatever reason, able to read them? Clearly if you write this kind of letter, you will know that other eyes will be upon it and you will write accordingly, not saying anything likely to cause offence. Equally, such letters may be written when you are perfectly well aware who the person is who will actually read the letter and you may take advantage of this to say what you want to say, obliquely, to that person. This applies particularly to letters sent to childen (see Chapter 5, page 68).

I am resigned

Not that many of us have to write resignation letters, except possibly when wishing to withdraw from employment (see Chapter 7, page 124). If we do, then such letters are usually best written, torn up and not sent.

But sometimes a resignation letter can be important in putting down in black and white and for the record precisely what has made you take the action. You will find writing this kind of letter very difficult, as many resignations occur in heated circumstances. It is therefore much better to see a resignation letter as simply something that fulfils whatever official or legal requirements there are (if any) so that you can withdraw from the job efficiently.

It is best not to go into any detail at all about your reasons for leaving – *however much you may want to*. Bitterness is difficult to hide and assuming an air of nonchalance won't help you one jot either. So, as always, be brief and to the point. The actual instrument of President Richard Nixon's unprecedented resignation in 1974 was matter-of-fact to the point of abruptness. He simply signed a letter to the Secretary of State, Henry Kissinger, which stated: 'I hereby resign the Office of the President of the United States.' No more, no less. Unfortunately, he became maudlin and self-justifying in his spoken utterances at about the same time.

Politicians usually make a meal of it. In British politics the exchange of letters between a Prime Minister and a minister who has either jumped of his own accord or been pushed is formalized and full of coded signals. The letters are quite openly intended for publication and traditionally contain certain well-worn phrases.

> Dear Prime Minister,
>
> You have told me that you would like me to resign, and this I willingly do . . .
>
> When we talked earlier today, you asked me if I would put my job at your disposal. This I am, of course, most happy to do . . . [Ha!]
>
> If it would help you in making these changes, I should of course be ready to place the offices I now hold at your disposal . . .
>
> I shall always be grateful for having had the honour of working with you and serving this government.
>
> Yours sincerely

If you are not leaving under a cloud (and even if you are), it is apparently worth while summarizing what you see as having been your achievements in office. This is useful public relations and could lead to your getting a few company directorships in the after life, as well as guiding the people who will have to write your political obituaries. Departing ministers are also prone to putting in the lines: 'May I take this opportunity to say how much I have appreciated being a member of your government' and 'I am very grateful to you for the many personal kindnesses you have shown me' – the latter suggesting, in particular, a level of intimacy that might impress others.

If, on the other hand, you have been caught up in some sex scandal, a 'personal statement' type of letter is called for. In this you must 'deeply regret any embarrassment that may have been caused' to the Government, your family and friends. You should almost certainly say that your 'wife and family are standing by you'. It is also possible to add, 'My own feelings at this time may be imagined' – but it is best to leave them that way.

Prime Ministers tend to write back like this:

Dear Eric,

I am sure you realize the need in the present situation for a broad reconstruction of the Government with a view to the future, and I am grateful to you for facilitating this . . .

You made it clear to me some time ago that your office was at my disposal whenever the circumstances became desirable. For private and family reasons you were beginning to feel the burdens of office too heavy. It was characteristic of you to write in this understanding way.

If Eric has been forced out office, the Prime Minister is brief but not curt, and adds: 'Your decision accords with the best traditions of British public life.'

Since I first gathered these materials for a book called *The Joy of Clichés* (1984), a new resignation reason has arisen, that the minister 'wishes to spend more time with my family'. Like all the rest, this should now be avoided. However, there is something to be said for the general tone of these phrases. They are dignified and suitable for a broad public audience. Though in parts self-serving, they are not whinging or whining. As such, they can be recommended at least as a model for 'tone of voice' in other fields of endeavour which may not even be public ones.

Letters to the editor

Newspapers and magazines thrive on the letters they receive from readers. It reminds them they are still alive, it helps fill up space at no cost, and it gives them ideas and topics for future articles.

At the bi-centenary of *The Times* in 1985 it was stated that the paper received about 55,000 letters a year – that is to say, letters specifically 'for publication'. This was claimed to be 'probably 10 per cent more than any other paper'. Subsequently, with the arrival of other quality papers like *The Independent* on the scene, I suspect there has been a decrease in this number – which is about a thousand a week – but still *The Times* correspondence column retains a certain cachet. It was King George V who, when asked by a friend for help in some matter, replied, 'My dear fellow, I can't help you. You'd better write to *The Times*.'

A little earlier, in 1968, a survey showed that though the number of letters written to *The Times* was 63,963, a mere 4,368 were actually published. These had been written by 436 dons and schoolmasters, 304 MPs, 182 clergymen, 156 peers and peeresses, 83 captains of industry, 39 bishops, and the remaining 3,070 by persons 'without titles or identification'.

So what are the qualities that enable letters to *The Times* – or indeed any other newspaper – to be published? They must be topical, well written, concise and exclusive to the paper – though quite often it is possible to find a letter that has been sent round all the papers and been printed in more than one.

Beyond this, there are virtually no rules. A good letter will get straight to the point and will have something original to contribute. That is all there is to be said.

Some people become quite addicted to the practice. A former Letters Editor of *The Times* related how some people wrote to the paper every day and some people even wrote five or six letters *a day*. Evidently, one South African gentleman wrote the same letter every day for thirty years 'on very expensive notepaper' . . . and sometimes he delivered it by hand.

Marked 'for publication'

There is a distinction between writing to the press 'for publication' and 'not for publication'. It may be that you wish to raise matters with an editor or journalist but in a letter which you do not wish them to publish in the paper. It is always important, therefore, when corresponding with journalists to make it clear what your intentions are. Marking your letter 'Not for publication' is a perfectly normal thing to do. Marking it 'For publication' is slightly pompous but avoiding any misunderstanding is still worth doing.

Signing on and off

But say you are writing to a newspaper for publication, how do you address the editor? Depending on the paper, you will find that whatever you write will get printed exactly as you wrote it, *or* will get rewritten to suit the paper's house style, *or* will be dispensed with completely.

For example, should you follow my general advice in the matter of writing to institutions and write 'Dear Editor' or 'Dear *Newspaper*' when writing to *The Newspaper*, you will find your copy replaced with 'Dear

Sir' and 'Yours etc.', as a matter of course. If you write to the London *Evening Standard* and other tabloids your 'Dear' and 'Yours' will be excised completely.

Like me, you may feel that 'Yours etc.' is not much of a way to end even the most mediocre epistle, but there it is. Only *The Independent* seems to allow letters to start with a Dr Johnson 'Sir:', but it does permit its correspondents to depart from Correct Form by ending 'Yours sincerely', 'Yours truly', 'Yours etc.', as they will. Likewise, *The Times* disciplines everyone to an initial 'Sir' while allowing whatever ending the correspondent requires – even such baroque variants as, 'I remain, dear sir, bemused' or 'Yours in stunned disbelief'.

'Writing letters to *The Times*, according to Barrie, is – or was in our young days – the legitimate ambition of every Englishman.' – Jerome K. Jerome, *My Life and Times* (1926)

Getting published

It is always difficult to explain to people why their letters have not been chosen for publication whereas others have, so many considerations come into play. 'For reasons of space' is the obvious one but cuts no ice when the space has been filled with other writers' lacklustre effusions.

To get your letter published it is essential that it deals with an issue already current in the newspaper or introduces a new one in a timely way. Beyond that, your letter has got to *say* something relevant (or entertaining) on an issue and doesn't just exist to enable you to get something off your chest.

If you are adding to a debate already under way, or responding to something you have spotted in the paper, it will make the letters editor's job easier if you make it plain what you are writing about. Some papers suggest you not only refer to the date of the article you are on about, but also put the page number. A great deal of time can be wasted hunting through back copies to find whatever it is a correspondent is alluding to, and this will not endear you to the editor.

Custom varies from paper to paper as to whether your letter will be acknowledged if it does not actually get published. Here is a letter I wrote to *The Times* in 1981:

Dear Sir,

The quotation that your new celebrated writer, Frank Johnson, gropes towards (April 27) is: 'Lord George-Brown drunk is a better man than the Prime Minister sober.' Far from being written at the 'height of the Brown Terror of the 60s', the remark was made on 6 March 1976; and, although Mr Johnson may well be righ in judging it to be a 'somewhat down-market observation', it appeared in a leading article of the newspaper that now employs him.

Yours faithfully

Possibly this was a bit near the knuckle, a mite too pointed, or simply not very interesting. A few days later came a 'bread and butter' note from someone whose signature I was unable to read, nor was it explained what position he/she held:

PRIVATE

Dear Mr Rees,

The Editor thanks you for the letter you kindly sent recently, and asks me to say that he has noted your comments carefully and with interest.

Yours sincerely

'Carefully and with interest' – ha! If the last bit sounds unlikely, it is nevertheless common practice on most newspapers to pass your letter on to the journalist who wrote the article you have written in about or to anyone in the office who might be interested.

Writing to the papers is a bit addictive and people do it for several purposes. I always noticed that when Graham Greene, the novelist, had a book coming out he would find some issue to write to the papers about, perhaps creating a little stir in the publicity pond.

I can't remember quite why I wrote the following letter to *The Times*. I expect it was because, as with my earlier effusion, I felt that a mistake (however trivial) should be corrected:

The Editor
The Times . . .   28th January, 1982

Dear Sir,

Your reporter (January 28) may not have been in a position to verify
his references but those of us who care about such things believe
that Beachcomber (J.B. Morton), not 'some anonymous wit',
deserves the credit for that felicitous line about 'the bourne from
which no Hollingsworth returns'.

Yours faithfully,

As I recall, this was the first letter to *The Times* that I had published.
Preceded by *'From Mr Nigel Rees'* and with a Johnsonian 'Sir', in place of
'Dear Sir', it went in precisely as I had written it, amazingly enough. It
certainly made its point briefly but – with hindsight – I can see that I had
assumed a manner ('. . . those of us who care about such things . . .')
which was a touch artificial.

What I had not anticipated was the spin-off reaction – not to what I
had written but to the fact that I had written at all. The *Times* did and
still does print the whole address of its letter writers (most other papers
now give an abbreviated version) which meant and still means that
other readers can write to the correspondent direct. As a result of the
above short letter I received various cheery notes from people I had not
seen for a while, one or two messages of support from lunatics, and an
offer to write a book.

Beware lunatics

Writing to the papers is an odd pursuit and attracts eccentrics in great
numbers. But sometimes the eccentricity lies on the part of the editor
who does not print letters like this:

                              from Lt. Col. A.D. Wintle
                                 The Royal Dragoons
                                    Cavalry Club
                              127, Piccadilly, W.1

To the
   Editor of
      The Times

Sir,

I have just written you a long letter.

On reading it over, I have thrown it into the wastepaper basket.

Hoping this will meet with your approval.

I am,
  Sir,
    Your Obedient Servant,

      A.D. Wintle

6 Feb. '46

This letter was not published and, although a favourite of editors, did not see the light of common day until 1985. Lunatics also flourish in the letters columns of local newspapers, or seem to. For some reason I still have a note of an extract from a letter to the *Birmingham Evening Mail* in May 1972, which someone drew to my attention:

> I think that the gentleman who created 'King Kong' would have been more gainfully employed in making a set of concrete steps at the Ashton Road end of Bracebridge Street to help old people get to the bus without having to make half-mile detours.

Indeed, letters to local papers are more likely to see the light of publication if they have a constructive point to make or have a surprise bouquet to hand out. This one – or something like it – recently appeared in a local London free-sheet in Kensington:

> I hope that you will find space to publish this letter as a suitable public tribute to JCB plc who have for so long been engaged in reinforcement and related works in the High Street. The very nature of the work over a protracted period has necessitated dreadful interruptions to traffic flow and the work itself has, on occasion, been very noisy.
>   The contract is nearly completed and from a ringside seat in my home which overlooks the site I have had first-hand experience of the work and it has been exemplary.

When seeking the rescheduling of some noisy work planned for nights and weekends, I have found cooperation to be forthcoming and I can testify to the company's continuing care and attention to the interests of residents most likely to be affected.

I know it is often fashionable to criticize the conduct of public works contractors. I would just like to record my thanks for the welcome standards shown by JCB plc.

Of course, not all letter writers to local papers are mad but it is probably harder for most of these people to escape the accusation that they are only writing for something to do, because they like the sound of their own voices and because they just love seeing their name in print. This may be unfair in many cases but should be borne in mind.

'Verbosa et grandis epistola' ('A wordy and grandiloquent letter'). – Juvenal, *Satires*, x.71 (*c.* 100 – *c.* 128)

More than a letter

A 'letter to the editor' can be rather more than a 'letter', of course. There is a certain type that is more of a manifesto or a form of political act. Keith Flett of London N17 who writes about thirty letters a week to newspapers (and has a surprisingly high acceptance rate) wrote (again) to *The Independent Magazine* (22 May 1993) to pooh-pooh the idea that letter-writing was 'a leisure activity, a hobby', as someone had earlier dismissed it. 'It is,' said Flett, 'a political intervention, often within an historical framework, in a medium which all too often has a very narrow focus on events.'

This assertion did not find acceptance among other *Independent Magazine* correspondents. One wrote, 'I rather suspect that the custom of letter-writing has diminished, which is why it is so easy for Mr Flett to be published.' Another dismissed the idea of letter-writing to newspapers as a 'political intervention': 'It is, surely, an ego-trip, pure and simple.'

This is an example, if ever there was, of the fate likely to befall all writers of letters to the press – they may get shot down, villified and ridiculed. Should they go so far as to get their facts wrong . . . well, public correction will not be slow in following.

Sometimes a newspaper letter *does* amount to something – a manifesto or 'political manifesto', indeed. In August 1961 John Osborne wrote from the South of France to *Tribune* what was headed 'A Letter to My Fellow Countrymen'. It was more like a slice of one of his dramas: 'This is a letter of hate. It is for you my countrymen. I mean those men of my country who have defiled it. . . . There is murder in my brain and I carry a knife in my heart for every one of you. Macmillan, and you, Gaitskell, you particularly. . . . Till then, damn you, England. You're rotting now, and quite soon you'll disappear. . . .' You get the drift?

My attention has been drawn . . .

Be careful about using the phrase, 'My attention has been drawn to the recent comments in your newspaper concerning . . .'. This suggests you are much too busy to read the papers yourself and have an operative to scan them for you. Or it might be taken to mean that you don't usually sully your hands by reading this particular rag yourself. If you want readers to think along these lines, then so be it, but better to get straight to the point and avoid any posturings.

Answering back

If you are attacked in a newspaper – and not just in the correspondence column – should you respond in kind with a letter to the editor? That is a tricky question and people who have been subjected to this form of Chinese water torture have thought about it long and hard. The wisdom that comes with age tells you that no response is invariably better than any which cannot be a guaranteed success.

A prominent (and much attacked person) in public life described to me the sensation of being got at in the public prints as like being 'mugged'. From my own experience of the matter, I can but agree, and yet it takes a very big person to be able *not* to reply to criticism wherever it occurs.

There is a terrible trap which makes you want to reply in a mildly facetious tone. For example, if pilloried in *Private Eye*, there is a temptation to write thus (as I once did), 'Dear Lord Gnome . . .' and so on. But this achieves nothing. Better to remain silent in a dignified manner, if you can manage it. Console yourself with the thought that today's newspapers will be wrapping tomorrow's fish and chips, and don't get rattled. Don't attempt to answer back, you will only get further embroiled. With newspapers it is impossible for you to have the last word or to get your point over in exactly the way you want it (even in a letter).

Dear Father Christmas

A sensitive topic. I am not going to provide a specimen letter for children to write to Santa Claus, but am merely going to remember something vaguely appropriate.

According to the *Sunday Telegraph* of 31 May 1987, John Peart-Binns, biographer of John Habgood, Archbishop of York, unearthed a letter written by Habgood when he was eight. 'Dear God,' it began, 'If you feel lonely up in the sky would you like to come down and stay with us? You could sleep in the spare room, and you could bathe with us, and I think you would enjoy yourself. Love, John'.

Addressed to 'Our Father Which Art in Heaven' it was opened by the Post Office and marked 'Return to sender', which, as Peart-Binns commented, has fewer theological implications than 'Gone away' or 'Unknown at this address'.

Fan mail

As Rita Carter recounted in her book entitled *Fan Mail* (1983), the comedian Benny Hill was puzzled to receive a batch of fan letters from Greece, all exactly the same, right down to the spelling mistake:

> Dear Benny,
>
> I'm one of your greatest fans and I'm living in Greece and I know that it would be rather difficult for you to send autographs abroad but my hottest dream is to have an autograph of you dedicated to me. Well, I give you all my admiration and I am waiting, impratiently, for my dream to come true.

Hill discovered that he was in receipt of the 'first-ever all-purpose, pro-forma fan letter', as it had been printed, in English, in a Greek fan magazine. All the fan had to do was insert the admired one's name and rattle it off. But who could resist being anyone's 'hottest dream'? I hope Benny Hill responded to every single one of them.

There is something quite admirable about writing a fan letter, if only because it is less worrying to the subject than some forms of fan worship. He or she can choose whether to reply and does not come under any pressure. Most people who receive fan letters answer them, however great the cost and however much work is involved. A secretary may have to be drawn in to help, and a certain element of the pro-forma reply may have to be introduced. But it is only proper that an expression of goodwill should be acknowledged. Pushy types and lunatics are soon spotted and ignored.

Aware of Benny Hill's experience, I am reluctant to suggest what a fan should write. But here is the first fan letter I ever received – from a schoolgirl following a performance in a play while I was still at university. It pleased me no end, I can tell you, and as you will gather, I still have it, complete with the interesting spelling.

SPECIMEN LETTER 51: FROM A FAN

Dear Mr Rees,

I first have a question to ask and then a plee. My question is are you going to go into acting as a carear? I thought you were great, and will I am sure make a great name for yourself. My friend —— and I both love acting and we hope some day to be able to go to a Drama School. —— is very good but with my figure and face! well I would rather not say!

Now my plee could you please, please hand round my programme to the cast and ask them to sign it (yourself as well of course) also the piece of blue paper I enclose for my friend ——.

Yesterday we wanted to come round to get your autographs but the mistress yelled at us hurry up so we had to go. I now write this letter to you imploring you to help me out of my dellema! Just try and imagine me down on my knees begging you to answer I would be now but it is so difficult to write kneeling down I find!!

Yours faithfully,

Very charming, even if the 'Yours faithfully' wasn't quite right with the 'Dear Mr Rees', nor did it sit very happily with the row of little kisses after the signature.

The clichés of fan letters are: when plunging in on first name terms, to say 'I hope you don't mind me calling you that, but I feel as if I already know you'; saying 'I think you are the best thing on TV', 'one needs a good laugh in these difficult times', 'please believe an ordinary housewife when she says . . .'; and ending with 'keep up the good work'.

Fan letters are not very popular if they require the recipient to expend any effort and asking for a photograph can be costly. Nowadays, however, autograph hunting and photograph soliciting tend to be very organized matters. A page from an autograph book is often sent by post, not forgetting a stamped addressed envelope for return. A self-addressed label is presented for the sending on of a photograph.

Rude letters

The non-fan letter is still very much with us. Probably there are more rude letters written to people in public life than letters of support. I am not sure. The people who write them hardly need coaching – the words just pour forth, so intent are the writers to get whatever it is that is bothering them off their chests. In 1906 Max Reger wrote what appears to be the original of a famous type of abusive letter to the music critic Rudolph Louis: 'I am sitting in the smallest room of my house. I have your review before me. In a moment it will be behind me.' Henry Ward Beecher (1813-87), the American Congregational minister and author, once arrived at a church and found a bundle of letters for him, one of which consisted solely of the word 'Fool'. He mentioned this in his sermon, adding: 'I have known many an instance of a man writing a letter and forgetting to sign his name, but this is the only instance I have ever known of a man signing his name and forgetting to write the letter.'

Sometimes, a letter is too slow a means of protest. Apparently, Sir Alec Douglas-Home, when he was Foreign Secretary, once received a telegram which said, 'TO HELL WITH YOU – OFFENSIVE LETTER FOLLOWS'.

Looking back through my files, I find that I have kept more anti- than pro- letters. Either this is because I have received more of the former, or possibly it is because they are so much more vivid . . .

Once I was delighted to receive a card addressed to:

Rees, the awful NOISE!
Radio 4,
BBC,
London W1.

Having made some innocuous comment about the theatre director, Peter Brook – to the effect that 'Whatever Peter Brook does is bound to be worth watching' – I rapidly received a fan letter (signed and with the sender's address, oddly enough) describing this as: 'A compliment paid by a small nonentity to a big nonentity.'

Encouraged by this response, I said some other things. Reactions was not slow in coming:

> Brighton
>
> Dear Friend, [ha!]
>
> I like your programme *Quote . . . Unquote* but I am constrained to warn you that your sarcastic and caustic remarks on biblical subjects ill become you – and these are heard by God – and 'HE is not mocked' (Galatians 6:7).
>
> I'm truly sorry that such a nice person as you seem to be should take this risk – the ultimate consequences of which you must be wholly unaware.
>
> Best wishes,

Here is another letter from a religious person, full of Christian charity, and in two colours of biro:

> I recall some few weeks ago your making an irreverent allusion to 'walking on the water' which means I shall never listen to your voice again if I can help it. However, for the general public who are supposed to be safeguarded by the BBC against anything which offends against good taste and decency, I recommend that, in future, you thoroughly rinse your mouth out with a good disinfectant before speaking on the radio.

In due course I involved myself with other people – Americans, even – in a programme which received a similarly warm reception:

> I find it exceedingly offensive because of the dirty-minded people taking part. *I wonder if their wives listen to it?* [my italics] It is highly objectionable to have hideous-voiced smut-loving Americans brought into the programme but homosexuality is too *dreadful* an affliction to be the subject for 'trying to be funny'. Are these unpleasant foreigners *paying* for their intrusion into *British* broadcasting? It is *more* than time this was put a stop to, and inquiries made . . .

And here is another, from a woman I had apparently brushed against without knowing it:

> Dear Nigel Rees
>
> I have just returned from the BBC Exhibition where I saw you a few yards in front of me. (I recognized your mouth from seeing it on *Countdown*.) Possibly recognition showed on my face – and I am well aware of the fact that I'm no beauty, but it would seem that I must be positively hideous because you literally fled before my very eyes!! I had no intention of devouring you – in fact I am not even attracted to you, as I would be to Sir Huw Wheldon! But I would have liked to say Hello. However, I know that I am a nonentity because I don't even work for the BBC. Perhaps it's only the less well known who are prepared to talk to the 'common herd' who only watch and listen but do not partake.
>
> Of course you won't remember so please don't write and apologize. I only wish that I were attractive, then you surely would have smiled, if not spoken.
>
> Best wishes,

The signer of this odd missive actually gave her address but, no, I did not write and pursue the matter. It all seemed very unreasonable, particularly when I am more than happy to talk to anybody, ugly or not, who has the nerve to approach me. Still, you could say that at least she was dealing with her problem in the least objectionable way, trying to work it out by writing a letter. A case, though, if ever there was one, for writing the letter but not sending it.

I could quote on, but won't. What amazes me is the pent-up fury of these correspondents. It is surprising, I suppose, that they have the time to spare in having a go at people such as myself. When each word they write has to be underlined several times and alternate lines written in different coloured inks, it must take quite some time. But I still marvel that they are willing to pay for a first-class stamp and take the trouble of walking all the way to the letter box just in order to sort me out.

On occasions, however, a rather touching strain emerges from such correspondence, even repentance. In 1977 I received this:

Dear Mr Rees,

I am writing to say how sorry I am to hear you taking part in such a beastly programme as *The Burkiss Way*. I put the radio on expecting to get the news. I had to listen to a silly disgusting entertainment – it was unfortunate for me that I was unable to reach the 'off' switch. The crudeness was bad enough. You might at least have had the decency to leave the Bible out of it. That half hour made me feel sick and my head has ached ever since.

Two years later, I happened to mention that letter in a *Woman's Hour* discussion on hate mail. Consequently, I got this from the same person, who had obviously heard the second broadcast, too:

Dear Mr Rees,

I am taking this opportunity to write and apologize for my letter sent some time ago. It was very unfortunate that your name was the only one I knew on that programme. Being an impulsive person I sat down at once and wrote that letter. I've since regretted that letter and wished to write, thinking only of the nicer side of you . . .

Very agreeable. Sometimes, too, correction can be done stylishly and gently:

St Andrew's, Fife

Dear Mr Rees,

Your programme *Quote . . . Unquote* is one of the wittiest on radio at this time but it would be even better if you could eliminate the slightly vulgar elements. I don't think I'm particularly puritanical but the people who listen to Radio 4 are pretty square and it is too cold up here to have much of a permissive society.

Last week I think you mentioned Lady Antonia Fraser. I haven't the faintest idea what she gets up to but the remark was in bad taste. It would be different if she had been dead 200 years. This letter needs no reply.

Most such letters need no reply. They are not written by reasonable people and entering into a correspondence with them (however much you may feel like giving them a piece of your mind) is neither worthwhile nor recommended.

But in certain circumstances you may feel an obligation to respond. It also depends on how combative a person you are. According to Russell Miller in the *Sunday Times Magazine* (26 August 1974), Tom Driberg, as a Member of Parliament, developed a deliberately infuriating technique to deal with the shoals of abusive letters he received. His secretary was instructed to reply, 'Tom Driberg asks me to thank you for your letter. He regrets he is unable to answer it individually, as he has had a great deal of correspondence on this subject; he is, however, most grateful for your support.'

Hateful letters

Serious hate mail, threatening mail, blackmail letters and poison-pen letters should be shown to other people and not kept to yourself. If necessary, such letters may be referred to the police for advice on dealing with them, possibly under the 1988 Malicious Communications Act.

'Hate mail is the only kind of letter that never gets lost by the Post Office.'
– Philip Kerr, *Dead Meat* (1993)

Even at a less threatening level, an anonymous letter is disturbing to receive. Letters should never be sent anonymously. Happily, newspapers will no longer print them, even under a pseudonym, as they once regularly used to do. They will, however, withhold your name and address if asked to do so and if there is good reason.

Round robins

A 'round robin' is a letter designed to bring a complaint to the attention of authority without divulging who has organized the signing. Originally used by sailors, it takes its name from the fact that the names of the signatories would be written in a circle so that the ring-leader(s) would not be apparent. (The word 'robin' is a corruption of 'ribbon' and has nothing to do with the bird.)

I doubt very much whether they exist today. The nearest thing we have, probably, is the letter to the newspaper with a host of distinguished signatories attached – but with the names in alphabetical order rather than in the round. Obviously, someone has to organize these. The fax machine has made the collating of signatures much simpler. Newspapers will probably carry out one or two checks on signatories to make sure that they have genuinely agreed to their names being attached.

Chain letters

There can be few more pointless, stultifying experiences than to receive what you immediately perceive to be a chain letter. You know the sort of thing, for which of us has not received such a thing?

WITH LOVE ALL THINGS ARE POSSIBLE

This paper has been sent to you for good luck. The original is in New England.

It has been around the world nine times. The luck has now been sent to you. You will receive good luck within four days of receiving this letter – provided you in turn send it out.

This is no joke. You will receive good luck in the mail. Send no money. Send copies to people you think need good luck. Don't send money as fate has no price. Do not keep this letter. It must leave your hands within 96 hours.

An R.A.F. officer received $470,000.

Joe Elliot received $40,000.00 and lost it because he broke the chain.

While in the Phillipines, Gene Welsh lost his wife 51 days after receiving the letter. He failed to circulate the letter. However, before her death he received $7,750,000.00.

Please send 20 copies and see what happens in four days. The chain comes from Venzuela [sic] and was written by Saint Anthony De Group, a missionary from South America. Since the copy must tour the world, you must make twenty copies and send them to friends and associates. After [a] few days you will get a surprise – this is true! Even if you are not superstitious.

Do note the following: Constantine Dias received the chain in 1953. He asked his secretary to make twenty copies and send them out. A few days later he won the lottery of two million dollars. Cerol Dadditt, an office employee, received the letter and forgot it had to leave his hands in 96 hours. He lost his job. Later after finding the letter again, he mailed twenty copies. A few days later he got a better job. Dalen Fairchild received the letter and not believing, threw the letter away. Nine days later he died.

In 1987 the letter was received by a young woman in California. It was very faded and barely readable. She promised herself that she would retype the letter and send it on, but she put it aside to do later. She was plagued with various problems, including expensive car repairs. The letter did not leave her hands for 96 hours. She finally typed the letter as promised and mailed them and got a new car.

REMEMBER, send no money. Do not ignore this letter.

ST. JUDE

It works.

I received this chain letter in October 1991. It appears to be in perpetual circulation, boosting post office revenues all over the world (and just possibly bringing people good luck). I know this because I received a more of less identical letter in November 1984! The only difference was that the earlier letter was typed in capital letters, the original copy was said to be in England rather than New England, the RAF officer received only $70,000, however Joe Elliot received $450,000. Gene Walsh lost his wife a mere six days after receiving the letter. I can perfectly well believe that the letter has been in circulation for forty years. I suppose one has to concede that it is an effective one, though the superstitious would probably respond even if it was written in greater gibberish.

Post scriptum

George Augustus Selwyn (d. 1791), the politician and wit, was one of those who believed that no woman could write a letter without adding a P.S. One day, a woman who had heard this, challenged him and promised to write the following day. Selwyn was delighted to find that after her signature she had added, 'P.S. Who is right now, you or I?'

(Malvolio:) 'Jove and my stars be praised! Here is yet a postscript.' – William Shakespeare, *Twelfth Night*, II.v.173 (1600)

'When he wrote a letter, he would put that which was most material into the postscript, as if it had been a by-matter.' – Francis Bacon, *Essays* No. 22 'Of Cunning' (1625)

'A woman seldom writes her mind but in her postcript.' – Richard Steele, in *The Spectator* (31 May 1711)

'The gist of a lady's letter is in the postscript.' – English proverbial saying (by 1801)

(Of Charles Lamb) 'His sayings are generally like women's letters; all the pith is in the postcript.' – William Hazlitt, *Conversations of Northcote*, 'Boswell Redivivus' (1830)

'What a girl! He had never in his life before met a woman who could write a letter without a postscript, and this was but the smallest of her unusual gifts.' – P.G. Wodehouse, *A Damsel in Distress* (1919)

There is a definite art in choosing what to consign to a postscript. If nothing else, when handwritten on a typed letter, the P.S. humanizes it.

Index